WHAT IS
LEAN SIX SIGMA?

Mike George

Dave Rowlands

Bill Kastle

McGRAW-HILL

New York   Chicago   San Francisco   Lisbon   London
Madrid   Mexico City   Milan   New Delhi   San Juan
Seoul   Singapore   Sydney   Toronto

Library of Congress Cataloging-in-Publication Data applied for.

30   QFR   21 20 19 18 17

ISBN 0-07-142668-X

Acknowledgments

Thanks to the following people for providing support and input in developing this book: Jim Buckman, University of Minnesota; Dick Cunningham, Johns Manville; Mike Gabler, Solar Turbines; Linda Garner, The Plaquesmith; Todd Graham, Johns Manville; Gloria Grohs, Director of Nursing (ret.); Roger Hirt, City of Fort Wayne; George Maszle, Xerox Corporation; Ashish Merchant, Western Union; Dina Mongelli, Xerox Corporation; Heather Presley, City of Fort Wayne; Tim Schwalm, Eastman Kodak; Lynn Sherman, Delafoil Inc.; Barry Shook, Xerox Corporation; Tom Vandini, Delafoil Inc. Thanks also to Sue Reynard, our editor and layout staff all-in-one, and Tonya Schilling and Lynn Rae Kastle, our proofreaders.

CONTENTS

A Note to Our Readers

People who have been in business for some time will probably recognize Six Sigma as one of the most widely used quality improvement methods available today. Those in manufacturing may have heard about Lean, a discipline that focuses on process speed and efficiency. To many others, "Lean" may sound like a dieting technique, and "Six Sigma" will simply be a number and a Greek word, with no particular meaning.

Either way, you're probably reading this book because your company is starting a Lean Six Sigma initiative. This book provides answers to some of your most important questions: What is Lean Six Sigma? Why is my company using it? What can it do for *me*?

First things first. What is Lean Six Sigma? Some people call it an improvement *method* because it uses data to identify and eliminate process problems. Others call it an improvement *engine* because it establishes a whole new set of roles and procedures inside an organization that work to continuously generate results. As you'll see when you read this book, both are right. Lean Six Sigma lives within a broader framework of meeting a company's goals and customer needs.

What you'll find in *What is Lean Six Sigma?*

The purpose of this book is to introduce you to Lean Six Sigma. It focuses on key themes, and is not intended as a reference manual. It shows how Lean Six Sigma helps companies flourish in a new world where customers expect high quality and fast delivery at minimal cost.

The first six chapters of this book walk through the foundations of Lean Six Sigma. The chapters emphasize the basic vocabulary and concepts you'll likely start hearing in your own company.

The last chapters look at applications of Lean Six Sigma. We provide evidence showing why so many companies are turning to Lean Six Sigma, and present case studies from teams of people just like you who have used the concepts and methods to improve their workplace.

Introduction:

What's In This For You

"There's money out there to be saved that you would not dream of when you start this," says Todd Graham. "That's the part I've really enjoyed—saving money for the plant."

Todd is an 18-year veteran of Johns Manville (JM), the only place he's worked since high school except for a brief stint as an auto mechanic. His career as a production/machine operator was going along smoothly until the late 1990s, when JM implemented what it called "variation reduction teams."

Though he had only a high school degree and a few college credits, Todd had always been interested in process improvement, so he applied to join a team and was accepted. Team members were pulled off their regular jobs, given some statistical training, and set to work. "Each variation reduction team made some progress," says Todd, "but they were really just a bunch of plant people struggling along. Nobody really knew what was going on in a broader sense."

That was about to change, however. In October 2001, Todd happened to see a JM newsletter that announced the company's intention to embark on something called Six Sigma. Todd recalls there weren't a lot of details given in the article, but it did mention the company was looking for people to volunteer to become something called "Black Belts," people who would be expected to manage projects at the plant locations. The article said that Black Belts would be required to commit at least two years to the job.

It sounded interesting to him, but Todd wasn't sure at first whether he wanted to get involved in the Six Sigma initiative. A month after seeing the notice, however, he was approached by management and asked to join the program, and he agreed. "What swayed me to become a Black Belt was the support I saw from the main headquarters," says Todd. "I thought that would mean we'd get much more support than we got on the variation reduction teams." As it turned out, he was right. "Top-down support has been really good," he says.

Soon after, Todd was officially relieved of his regular job responsibilities as he embarked on the first of five weeks of training. "The first week was all about leadership," he explains. "Then we did four weeks of additional training, spaced about a month apart. We'd get a week of training, then go back into the plant to work on a project, come back for more training, return to the project, and so on."

Todd describes his work on the training project as a real eye opening experience. "We didn't realize it would be so difficult to get useful data," says Todd. In the process he was studying, a number of raw products are melted together to make glass. The team's goal was to make the process and product more consistent, so they wanted to measure how well the materials were blended before and after transport. "It could take two or three weeks to get the samples analyzed," Todd says. "That meant that data I was looking at on any given day reflected what was happening three weeks ago. That didn't help me manage what's going on now."

Ultimately, he says, the team was able to solve only some of the data issues. They reached perhaps 40% of the original goal for the project. "What I learned is that projects have to be scoped properly," he adds. To that end, JM's insulation division recently brought together all of its Black Belts for a two-day course on project selection and screening.

Since he completed his training in April of 2002, Todd's work life has been both interesting and challenging. "The upside is that it's been a lot of fun, especially if you enjoy working with people and statistics and understanding processes," he says. "But it's a lot of work up front to learn all this stuff. Most of the statistical tools and concepts came pretty easily to me, but there's a lot of material presented in a short amount of time."

His first year had additional challenges, he adds, because of great demands placed on the JM Black Belts. "We were doing most of the project work ourselves, as well as trying to coach and mentor other people involved in Six Sigma," says Todd. Now, he continues, the company is developing more Green Belts, people who receive basic training—though not as much as Black Belts—and can participate on projects. That means the Black Belts can focus more on acting as internal consultants, guiding teams in their work, and helping them select the right data tools to use.

"What's been great is that we're seeing good results company wide. I think the net benefits were three or four million dollars within JM last year," says Todd. "There's a lot of low hanging fruit out there if you know where to look."

Todd's story is typical of people who get involved in Lean Six Sigma by becoming Black Belts. They find the experience both challenging and rewarding on a number of levels.

Some readers of this book will face choices much like Todd did about whether to go through extensive training and leave their regular jobs to become Black Belts. Many of you may be required to go through basic Lean Six Sigma training. But even if your participation in training is required, you will still have to decide for yourself how actively you want to support Lean Six Sigma in your company.

The purpose of this book is to give you enough background information so you can start making these decisions for yourself.

Making the case

The best argument we can make to convince you to not just read this book but to get involved with Lean Six Sigma is that there is very little downside. We understand that many companies have tried other improvement efforts in the past only to see them fail. So it's not surprising that many people will be skeptical about Lean Six Sigma. But even if the worst happens, and ultimately the efforts go nowhere, the kind of training and education offered through Lean Six Sigma can only enhance your job skills.

The second-best argument for getting involved in Lean Six Sigma is that the upside is enormous. By using Lean Six Sigma in your own work area, you can...

- Help your company become more profitable
  - Grow revenue
  - Cut costs
  - Improve delivery time
  - Reduce inventory
  - Increase customer satisfaction
- Develop valuable job skills such as...
  - Decision making
  - Problem solving
  - Teamwork
- Make your own job and workplace work better
  - Get rid of a lot of waste—which will save you time and make your work more meaningful

In their own words

We talked to a range of people whose companies had started using Six Sigma or Lean Six Sigma. Here's what a few of them told us about getting involved:

- From Heather Presley of the City of Fort Wayne: "Don't get involved unless you're completely committed to making the end result happen. There were days I would look at that process and think there was no way we could get the kind of results we were looking for. It really takes tenacity. But you also don't have to fight all the fights alone." She also comments that, "If your organization is always going for the big win, they will probably have quite a few failures. But if you get people trained to THINK in terms of process improvement, they'll be better employees."

- Ashish Merchant joined Western Union right out of business school just a few years ago. He works in their international money transfer business, a rapidly growing unit within Western Union. In 2002, he was offered the chance to go through Green Belt training. "I saw quickly that this was not rocket science. It has a lot of common logic, but it's also a disciplined approach." He notes that "Some people teach Six Sigma like it's gospel. But that's not a good approach. You need to go through the discipline but use what's right for your project. Don't leave common sense at the door." He's also discovered that he can apply what he's learned on the job everyday. "You can improve productivity remarkably on-the-job by using even simple methods."

- Barry Shook, a manager at Xerox, moved out of manufacturing into the business services arm of the company. He's seen that practicing Lean and Six Sigma techniques has not only

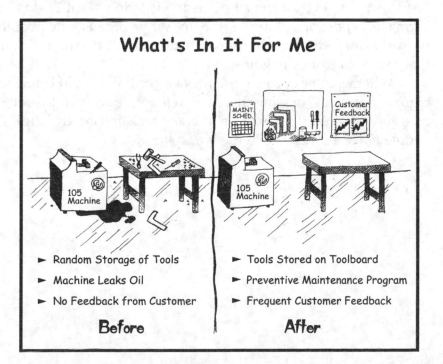

improved their operations, but is also becoming a competitive edge in his business. "One of our clients recently decided to introduce Six Sigma methods in their company. So they're looking for vendors who know what Six Sigma means and have incorporated it into their own environment," he remarks. "For each and every one of us to be successful, it is our responsibility to provide our customers with world class service. That doesn't mean being reactive, that means being proactive. Lean Six Sigma gives you the steps, tools, and methodology to take you to that level."

Conclusion

We can't guarantee that your company's Lean Six Sigma efforts will be successful, or that they'll last. But the kind of gains that companies—and their customers—see make it very difficult for them to pull back. In city government, for example, there is a very real possibility that the leadership could completely change as often as every four years. But as Heather Presley remarked, "At this point, even if the city decided it didn't want to do Six Sigma any more, it's going to remain. Why? Because the people we serve are getting used to much better service from the city. If that disappears, they're going to notice."

Whether or not you choose to get more involved in Lean Six Sigma afterwards, reading this book will introduce you to methods and concepts that have a *proven* track record in helping people make a difference in the workplace.

PART 1

FOUNDATIONS OF
LEAN SIX SIGMA

CHAPTER 1

The Four Keys to
Lean Six Sigma

Bank One is a national company with branch offices in many states. Each month, its National Enterprise Operations staff handles more than 200,000 requests from customers who want to get copies of old checks. Data from early in 2000 showed that on a monthly basis, anywhere from 10% to 25% of these requests were *not* filled to the customer's satisfaction. Often the copies were late, or unreadable, or the original couldn't even be found.

And it wasn't just the customers who were unhappy. How would you like to be one of the service staff having to handle all the complaint calls they got?

Time after time, the bank had tried to solve the problem, but with no lasting results. Then, when the company embarked on a new initiative based on Lean Six Sigma methods, management decided that the check retrieval process was one of the first things they should tackle.

This time around, the approach to solving the problem was very different. For one thing, people representing each part of the check retrieval process were brought together. The team included frontline staff who received the requests, people responsible for locating the filed original or microfiche copy, as well as some who mailed the photocopies. (In the past, it's the people who received the requests who took most of the blame for problems.) Secondly, the team also got a lot of support from coworkers who had a lot of experience in making improvements.

Thirdly, the team didn't just rely on their opinions about what the problem was. They used a problem-solving method that required them to

1) Use their creativity to think about the problem in new ways.
2) Collect data to see if what they thought was happening was true. In some cases, their theories turned out to be right. But they also discovered a number of issues they hadn't even thought about before, such as problems with vendors who processed the microfiche film. The data also helped them identify which issues caused the most problems.
3) Develop solutions that they could show would solve the issues they had confirmed with data.

The team ended up making changes in nearly every step of the process. For example, the clerks who took the requests from customers got better training, including how to fill out the request forms correctly and completely. The staff who processed the microfiche film started operating under new procedures for maintaining equipment. As a result, service failures are now just a third of what they used to be (about a 66% reduction from the peak)... and service staff are happy that they have far fewer angry customers calling!

This case study highlights the foundations of Lean Six Sigma, as shown in Figure 1.1 (next page). Above all, the team was working on a problem that was important to their company and its customers. In addition...

- Their goal was to **delight customers**— delivering higher quality service in less time.

- To achieve that goal they had to **improve their processes.** To do that, they had to eliminate defects (anything that was unacceptable to a customer) and focus on how the work flowed through the process.

- The people who work in the different process areas used **teamwork**, sharing ideas with each other so they could solve the problem.
- All their decisions were **based on data.**

Figure 1.1:The Keys to Lean Six Sigma

It took all of the elements, working together, to create real solutions. Any of the elements alone isn't enough. You need to *combine* the creativity of people working on the process with data and with an understanding of customers and processes. The next four chapters of this book walk through each of these elements in more detail and show how they apply to your own job.

CHAPTER 2

Key #1:
Delight Your Customers
with Speed and Quality

It used to be that a company would decide what features to include in its products or service based solely on what their engineers or marketing staff said they should be doing. And people were taught that the only opinion that really mattered was the boss's.

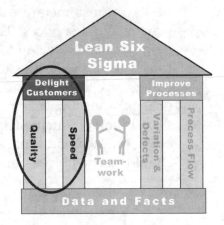

Nowadays, those old-fashioned notions have been replaced by a new attitude that only customers can define quality. The logic seems obvious when you stop to think about it. Customers are the people who will decide whether to spend their money on your company's services or products. They'll be comparing your offerings against everything else in the marketplace and determining which ones best fit their needs. (That's why Lean Six Sigma projects always start by trying to figure out what it is your customers will be focusing on as they compare you to your competitors.)

In the hotel business, for example, "quality" to some customers will mean a five-star hotel. To others, it will mean a lower-priced motel that's clean and close to a highway. In the auto business, quality can mean anything from a Lexus to a small wagon that gets good mileage. In manufacturing, it might mean having goods delivered in small batches twice a week, or meeting very narrow specifications. It all depends on what the customer wants. The companies who will do best in the marketplace are those who take the time to see everything through their customers' eyes and deliver what *they* want.

It's not just these external customers—people outside your company—whose opinions matter, either. You have internal customers, too. Those are the people inside your company to whom you hand off your work. Have you ever asked these internal customers what they want from you? What is most important to them in the information or service or product you provide?

In Six Sigma, you'll hear the term **Voice of the Customer** or "VOC" all the time. It's used to indicate that the opinions and needs of customers are being represented in decisions about products and services. There is a mix of VOC techniques that help companies live up to the ideal of meeting or exceeding customer needs. Some are simple, like tracking complaint calls that come in. Others are more complex, such as setting up focus groups or visiting customer sites.

Whatever methods you use, the biggest obstacle is developing the awareness that any decision about a service or product should start with customers.

What's Wrong With This Picture?

The goal: eliminate defects

Since Lean Six Sigma starts with customers, its goal is clear—to eliminate anything that doesn't meet their needs. In Lean Six Sigma terms, things that don't meet customer needs are called **defects**. So if you promise a 3-day turnaround time and it takes you 3.5 days, that's a defect. If you're entering a purchase order and enter the wrong product code, that's a defect. If you're producing lamps and the wiring is frayed, that's a defect.

One of the challenges you'll face as you begin to use Lean Six Sigma is defining and measuring defects. For example, suppose you find out your customers want courteous service. How would you determine whether or not they got it? The thing to keep in mind is what aspects of your product or service are most important to your customers. Then find ways to determine whether or not you've met those needs. If you don't, your process is probably producing defects.

What's also important in Lean Six Sigma is checking on the consistency in your products, services, and processes. How likely is it that customers will consistently get something they're happy with? If you deliver what they want one day, but not the next day, they may take their business elsewhere.

Defining "customers"

Six Sigma takes a broad view of what a "customer" is. It includes the people outside your company who purchase your services and products AND the people inside your company who use the output of your work.

Even if you have little contact with external customers—people outside your company—keep in mind that they are the ultimately judges of your company's products or services. They're the ones who determine whether your company will be profitable.

So even if you're assigned to improve processes just in your own work area, ask the question "Would doing this just be nice for us, or would it ultimately help our paying customers?"

The links between quality, speed, and low cost

Most of us can identify with "customers needs" because all of us are customers, too. We want the same thing our company's customers want: quality, speed, and low cost. When we order a product or service, we want it delivered as quickly as possible and on time (**speed**), with no errors (high **quality**), and at the lowest possible price (low **cost**).

What few people realize before they begin studying Lean Six Sigma is that we can't really achieve any of these goals without doing all of them at the same time. Why?

1) A process that makes a lot of errors cannot keep up its speed. **So high quality makes it possible to attain fast speed.**

2) A process that works slowly is prone to errors (low quality). To some people, that sounds like it doesn't make sense: don't people make *fewer* mistakes if they work slowly? The key here is that we're looking at overall process speed, not how quickly an individual person or machine works.

   Imagine following some item in your process from beginning to end. How much time is it actually worked on? How much time does it spend sitting around *waiting to be worked on?* In the vast majority of cases, "work" spends most of its time waiting. This waiting time is easy to see in manufacturing plants where material is stacked to the ceiling. If you're in service areas, you have inventory, too—it's just harder to see! How many e-mails or voicemails or work requests do you have in your computer or on your desk waiting to be worked on?

   Bad things happen to work that sits around waiting. In manufacturing, materials can become outdated or damaged. In services, information can get outdated.

   The lesson? **You have to do the things that create process speed (meaning "eliminate delays") if you want to achieve the highest levels of quality.**

3) Low quality and slow speed are what make processes—and services and products—expensive. For example, if you have "inventory" of any kind—products or materials or requests for information or customer orders—that has to sit around before it's worked on, that means there is unfinished work that your company has spent money creating but can't yet bill to the customer. **So the only way to consistently offer the lowest price—and still make a profit!—is to improve quality** *and* **speed.**

It's because of these links that Lean Six Sigma offers advantages over other improvement methods. Traditionally, the methods we now call "Six Sigma" focused more on quality than speed. The methods known as "Lean" are better at improving process flow and speed than on improving quality. Combining the two is what makes Lean Six Sigma such a powerful improvement tool.

A mini-case study

To see how the concept of customers and defects apply in business, let's look at a story inspired by a real company:

Meet the folks at Sigma Oil Change

The managers at Sigma Oil Change are concerned about stiff competition from both other "quick lube" franchises and from automotive garages that want to recapture the oil-change business they've lost.

They began their work correctly by listening to the Voice of the Customer—finding out what their customers want. One thing they realized early on was that they actually have two different types of customers: (1) individual consumers bringing in family cars, and (2) fleet operators regularly bringing in cars owned and operated by companies. Determining whether these different customers had different needs was one of their initial goals.

A survey of both types of Sigma Oil Change customers exposed what Lean Six Sigma calls **Critical to Quality** (CTQ) requirements. These are the features of a product or service that are MOST important to your customers, the ones you should pay close attention to. Any defects associated with CTQ requirements can be fatal to a business. In this case, the CTQs for both groups included...

√ using the right oil and filter
√ timely service (in and out within 20 minutes)
√ refilling fluids as needed
√ checking/fixing tire inflation
√ providing a comfortable, clean waiting area
√ providing friendly service
√ tightening all caps to prevent leaks between visits

In addition, the fleet customers wanted Sigma Oil Change to produce monthly reports on services for all their vehicles.

On the one hand, nothing on this list was particularly surprising. But having a confirmed list of specific customer needs gave the team a focus for their improvement efforts. (And in many cases, you *will* find some surprises on such lists.) Within a few months, the company made progress on being able to *consistently* deliver what their customers wanted, which led to an increase in repeat business—and increased profits in a competitive market.

What it means to focus on customers

Developing a focus on customers means a lot more than just doing a survey now and then. It means developing an awareness that customer needs should shape most of the work we do every day.

Mark Saloman works for the Neighborhood Code Enforcement Department in Fort Wayne, Indiana. Early in one improvement project, an expert who was coaching the team asked Mark the following question: "Who are you really working for? Who is your customer?"

Mark thought about it for a while, and said, "I think it's the Citizen's Review Board. That's who I report to."

"Okay," said the expert, "the Citizen's Review Board. Let's pursue that. If they're your customer, what do they do?"

"Well, they review my code enforcement write-ups about which people are violating the code," said Mark.

"So to satisfy your customer, all you have to do is go write up a bunch of reports and send them to the review board?" asked the expert. "That's all you need to do to meet your goals?"

"Well, no," Mark answered.

The expert then asked, "What's the goal of code enforcement?"

"To improve the neighborhood," said Mark.

"So who is really your customer?"

"I guess it's the people in the neighborhood," Mark said.

Mark's original answer is similar to what most people would say—that it was "their boss" that they needed to be concerned about. Being concerned about what your manager wants is a fact of life in business. But in Lean Six Sigma organizations, what the *manager* wants is to make customers happy. He or she therefore takes on the role of encouraging a customer focus among employees. Mark, for example, made some changes in his procedures once he realized who his customers were. He started making direct contact with citizens, attending neighborhood association meetings, and so on. This not only helped him focus on projects of importance to Fort Wayne residents, but led to greater understanding and cooperation from his constituents.

Conclusion

Having a true customer focus is not something you do only during an improvement project. We should all make a conscious effort to check what we're doing against what our customers want. We need to know what it will take to delight these customers—what they would define as "quality" work, how quickly they want our products or services delivered, what they would see as a "defect," and so on.

CHAPTER 3

Key #2:
Improve Your Processes

Once you understand your customers, the next step is figuring out a
way to get better at delivering what
they want. The answer lies in
improving the processes your company uses to generate the services
and products you sell.

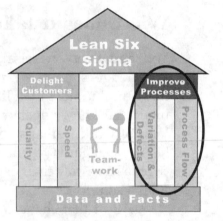

Dr. W. Edwards Deming, an
American statistician who led the
quality movement in Japan (and later
in America), spent much of his time
trying to convince people that most
quality problems are "in the process, not the person." For most of
his 60+ year career, he promoted his 85/15 rule, based on his
experience that 85% of problems were *built into* the way work
was done (and hence under the control of management). Only
15% of the problems, he said, were really the fault of individual
employees.

Most frontline employees had no trouble accepting
Dr. Deming's assertions. After all, they were the people who paid
the price for a lack of training, poor equipment, little communication, and unrealistic goals. In short, they worked under conditions that *guaranteed* poor quality. It was often *managers* who
resisted Dr. Deming, because they were trained to find "who to
blame" when something went wrong.

In the last few years of his life, Dr. Deming admitted his
85/15 ratio was probably wrong. More than likely, he said, it's
96% of problems that are built into the work *system*. Individual
employees, he concluded, could only control perhaps 4%!

Why does it matter if most problems are "in the system"? Because it means that if you want to improve quality, you have to change the way work is done. That's why Lean Six Sigma focuses on process improvement. In fact, the purpose of most improvement efforts is to use data to find out what's wrong in the system that allows the problems to happen in the first place. Removing these problems will allow your company to provide better products and services to customers.

What does it take to improve processes?

You and everyone else reading this book has some process knowledge, simply as a result of performing your job day in and day out. But more than likely, you've never been asked to document that knowledge, or discuss it with others doing the same kind of work. Perhaps no one has ever used the term "process" before in regards to your work. When something goes wrong, people have only their experience and trial-and-error to come up with a solution.

All of that changes with Lean Six Sigma. There is a great deal of emphasis on:

- Documenting how work gets done (the steps that comprise the process)
- Examining the *flow* of work between people or workstations
- Giving people the knowledge and methods they need to constantly improve that work

There are a lot of different process improvement methods, some of which are covered later in this book. But almost all of them serve one of two purposes:

- To **eliminate variation** in quality and speed (a major source of defects)
- To **improve process flow and speed**

The majority of process improvement work you'll ever do falls into one of those two categories, so we'll spend a little time explaining what each of them means.

Eliminate variation

We all know at a gut level that nothing is exactly the same day in and day out. Some days it takes you longer to get to work than others. Some restaurant customers get served in 10 minutes, other take twice that or more.

Everything varies. What's important is that the *way* in which something varies—the patterns in the variation—can expose the cause of problems and point the way towards solutions.

The language around variation is what gave rise to the term "six sigma." Those of you new to improvement may not have heard that term before. The Greek word "sigma" is used in statistics to stand for **the amount of variation** seen in a process, a set of data, or anything you can measure.

To illustrate the concept, look at the two charts in Figure 3.1. Each point represents a single measurement taken on a process.

Figure 3.1: Variation in process outputs

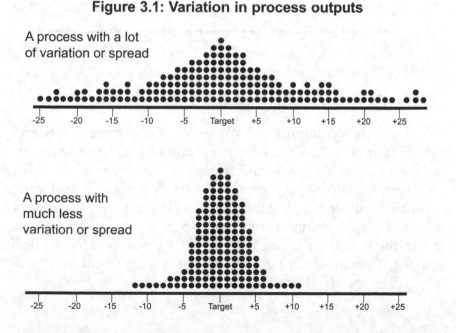

For our purposes here, it doesn't really matter what the measurements are—they could be delivery times, weights, lengths, customer satisfaction scores, etc. What's important is that the top chart shows a process with a lot of variation or spread. The bottom chart shows a process with much less variation.

Variation defines the "sigma" level

Why is variation important? We've taken the same charts and added lines to indicate what the customer *wants* (their ideal **target**), and what they will find acceptable. (See Figure 3.2.) For example, a customer expecting delivery "by noon" (the target) might actually be happy if the package arrives anywhere from 11 a.m. to 1 p.m. A manufacturer that is purchasing 1000 gallons of paint (the target), might be satisfied if the delivery is 995 to 1005 gallons. (In manufacturing, the range of acceptable values is usually called **specifications**.)

Figure 3.2: Variation affects our ability to meet customer needs

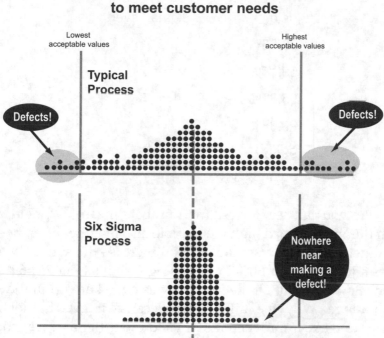

Recall from the last chapter that anything that doesn't meet customer needs is a "defect." When you compare the process performance against what customers want, you can see that the process with a lot of variation, like the one in the top chart, is going to produce a lot of defects—and disappoint a lot of people! If your processes are like this chart, your customers will view them as unpredictable. Sometimes they'll get what they want, but a lot of times they won't.

In contrast, the bottom chart shows a process that operates with very little variation. As you can see, all the data points are clustered tightly around the center. Such a process rarely misses when it comes to meeting customer needs! Customers will view it as very reliable.

So where does the "sigma" term fit in? The table at the top of the next page shows the link between process yields (the number of goods or services that are good enough to be sold to customers) and sigma numbers.

Table 3.1: Sigma Numbers and Yields

Yield	Sigma Level
30.85%	1
69.15%	2
93.32%	3
99.38%	4
99.977%	5
99.99966%	6

As you can see, low sigma numbers mean low yield, and high numbers mean a high yield. Note also that the differences in yield get smaller and smaller as you increase the sigma level. It takes a jump of over 30% in yield to go from sigma 2 (=69%) to sigma 3 (=93%). But all the sigma levels over 4 are up in the 99% yield range. Why the difference? Because it gets harder and harder to make improvements in yield the better a process operates. In other words, it's relatively easy to make improvements in a bad process—one with a sigma of 1 or 2—but very difficult to improve a process that is already working fairly well.

Fixing the process is what improves sigma levels

Now here's one of the secrets of Lean Six Sigma: in order to have an *outcome* with very little variation (like the bottom chart in Figure 3.2), **everything leading up to that point has to work well, too.** This explains why Lean Six Sigma focuses so much on process improvement. You need to make the work in your area more reliable, more predictable to reach high levels of quality—which means eliminating variation.

For a real example of how businesses can capitalize on reduced variation, just think about FedEx. It created a new industry because of its ability to *reliably* meet promised delivery dates. If their "guarantee" of 10:00 a.m. delivery had really meant "anytime tomorrow," how long do you think they would have stayed in business? People keep coming back because they can count on having their packages delivered by the guaranteed time. FedEx's experience also shows that reducing variation is something that both service and manufacturing businesses should focus on.

Improve process flow and speed

Variation is one of the most common sources of problems in a process. But another source is how the work flows through the process—the hand-offs from one person or workstation to another, the *physical* path that the work follows in an office or on the factory floor. Here's just one example…

> Bank One uses what they call their "wholesale lock-box" process to handle business-to-business payments (where one company is paying another company). These payments often arrive at Bank One in overnight express packages. The deposits can be as large as several million dollars, so obviously the customers want fast service!
>
> Originally, an overnight pack had to travel one-and-a-half miles inside the Bank One office just to make it through every step of the process! It would go to one office, then down the hall to another, then up the elevator to a third, then down to yet another office, and so on.
>
> Don't believe it? Neither did the Lockbox staff at first. But then as they traced the process—following the *flow* of the work—everyone was floored. "Well, I guess maybe it *could* travel that far!"
>
> What was even more astonishing was just how much that distance could be shortened. The team applied Lean Six Sigma methods they'd just learned to document how the process currently worked, then used structured creativity techniques to think of a better way to lay out the process. They looked at process changes (altering the process steps) as well as redesigning the physical flow by moving offices and workspaces.
>
> Soon, they ended up with a workspace design that required just 386 walking steps to complete the entire process (an 80% reduction in "travel").

This lockbox service at Bank One had a promised turnaround time of 4 hours. (Deposits in by 8 a.m. would be credited by noon; in by 11 a.m., credited by 3 p.m., etc.) Since some of these deposits could be worth a million dollars or more, the short turnaround time was considered essential from the customers' viewpoint. If you were Bank One, would you feel more confident about delivering within the timeframe if the deposit only has to travel 386 steps, or if it has to travel more than 1.4 miles?

This case from Bank One illustrates the importance of paying attention to process flow, both the **physical path** that work travels and the **process steps** required. One of the best ways to speed up a process is to eliminate process steps that aren't really necessary—meaning they don't meet a customer need. Another way is to redesign how work flows in the workspace.

That's why teams often spend the early part of an improvement project drawing a map of the process, either a drawing of the physical layout or a "flowchart" that shows the process steps. The teams have to examine every step and ask "Is this step necessary? What value does it add to our customers?"

Here's an example: The engineering department at one company was criticized for taking too long to implement design changes in their products. When they studied the process, the team discovered that approvals were needed from *seven* different managers. So the change notice would go to one manager, sit in the in-box for a few days, eventually get reviewed, then passed on to the next manager… where it would sit in another in-box for days, and so on. No wonder it took weeks to get approved!

When the team looked more closely at the purposes of having all seven signatures, they realized that five of the managers had no particular expertise they could contribute to the process. The team therefore changed the process so that only two approvals were needed. (The other five managers were sent copies of the design change notices because knowing something was in the works was helpful to them, but their signature was not required to approve the change.) Now it takes less than a week for the two remaining managers to review the form, resolve any issues, and set the rest of the process in motion. The product re-design process goes much more quickly, and customers can get improved products much faster than they used to.

Later in this book (Chapter 7), we'll show examples of the concepts and improvement tools that can help expose process flow problems.

Get rid of the waste in processes

It is standard in medicine for every surgeon to specify his or her own surgical tray of instruments and supplies for any procedure. In the cardiac surgical unit at Stanford Hospital & Clinics, that meant there were six different surgical trays for each type of case, one for each surgeon.

A central theme of Lean Six Sigma, however, is that unnecessary complexity adds cost, time, and enormous waste. So Stanford got all the surgeons together and asked "can't we get rid of some of these options?" Naturally the surgeons were skeptical at first: "We each need our own surgical tray."

But was that really true? When pushed to examine the issue more closely, the surgeons realized that having six different trays had little impact on the *quality of care provided to patients.* Within the space of a few meetings, they were able to agree on a standard surgical tray. That meant the purchasing department had to buy fewer types of instruments, and could make better deals by buying the larger quantities of the instruments they still used.

Stanford went on to apply this simplicity principle and other Lean Six Sigma concepts throughout the hospital. The result? Annual material costs dropped by $25 million. Care costs dropped as well: for example, the average total cost of Coronary Artery Bypass Graft surgery fell by 40%, and mortality rates dropped from 7.1% to 3.7% in the cardiac surgical unit.

Put yourself in Stanford's shoes, and it's likely you would have approached the problem much more traditionally, trying to prepare the surgical trays faster or better rather than asking whether all those trays were necessary in the first place.

But under Lean Six Sigma, much of what is now accepted as "just the way work happens" is recognized for what it really is—**waste**. All organizations need to develop Stanford's willingness to challenge themselves: "Which of these costs improve patient outcomes, and which don't?" And it's that type of critical thinking that's key to seeing big gains.

Conclusion

Process improvement is the *only* way to improve the results that your company wants to improve. You have to examine how work flows from one person or workstation to the next. You have to look at variation and how it affects the process.

And above all, you need to become a "process thinker"—someone who frames problems and issues in terms of what may be happening in the process. Making this mental leap has a much more profound effect than it may sound at first.

Suppose, for example, that some item of work in your area—a report, an order, a part assembly—was completed late or done incorrectly. The natural tendency for all of us is to look for *who* to blame, to find the *person* who is at fault.

It's true that all of us mess up from time to time. But a process thinker assumes, rightly so, that *most* of the time the problem arose because of the process. He or she will ask questions like, "Was there clear communication to the person about what was expected? Did that person have all the information, materials, equipment, etc., needed to perform the job correctly? Was that person trained properly in how to do that work? What are the critical factors that allowed the goof-up and how can we prevent it from ever happening again?"

You'll know that you've become a process thinker the first time a problem arises and you think first "what's going on in the process" rather than "that person really screwed up again!"

CHAPTER 4

Key #3:
Work Together for
Maximum Gain

In today's business world, having people work together to improve processes and solve problems is not a luxury. It's a necessity. Remember the Bank One "check retrieval" case told at the beginning of Chapter 1? The problems with that process had existed for a long time. They had proven "immune" to previous improvement efforts. Bank One finally solved the biggest problems by bringing together people from all 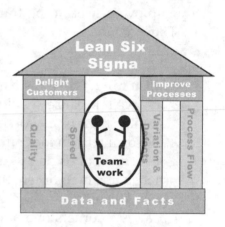 parts of the process and different departments and having them use data, facts, and process knowledge to get at the root causes.

In a Lean Six Sigma company, teamwork doesn't just mean having formal teams make improvements, though that's part of the picture. Another part is having an environment where people are encouraged to work together every day. People discuss and resolve problems openly rather than behind closed doors; they don't use issues as ammunition for attacking each other.

There is a feeling of "we're all in this together." People are enthusiastic about sharing and learning from each other. Meetings are energized, productive—and the real meetings happen *in* the meetings, not in the hallways or on the shop floor afterward. Information is shared openly and freely, even "bad news" because it's understood that hiding or distorting information won't lead to real improvement.

Does this sound too good to be true? It's certainly different from what most of us are used to, but organizations who have encouraged teamwork have reaped the benefits.

Getting good at working together: the skills of collaboration

Placing high value on having people work together is something new in many organizations. It's not enough for managers to simply tell people to collaborate. There are specific skills that all employees need to be trained in to have *effective* collaboration. They include:

1) **Listening skills:** Listening is something most of us think we do well, because we do it all the time. We listen to spouses, family, friends, coworkers, managers, store clerks… everyone we deal with in the course of a day. But despite all of this practice, most of us don't know how to listen well, *especially* when tension is high or tempers are about to flare. Learning how to use listening to really understand what people are trying to say is a cornerstone of effective collaboration. Part of "listening" includes developing inquiry skills so you can draw information out of your teammates. (You'll also need good "advocacy" skills, being able to clearly state your own ideas and support them with facts and observations, but most of us are better at that than we are at listening.)

2) **Brainstorming & discussion techniques:** One of the reasons for having people work in groups is to tap into everyone's ideas and knowledge. There are a lot of fun brainstorming techniques that get people to think creatively. And discussion techniques can help groups make sure that everyone gets a chance to be heard.

3) **Organizing ideas:** If you do a good job at listening, brainstorming, and discussion, many times you'll end up with a long list of ideas. If you have a list of 50 solution ideas for a

problem your team is working on, what do you do with them? In most cases, it's not practical or efficient to pursue each suggestion one-by-one. That's why collaboration techniques include methods for sorting through, organizing, and prioritizing ideas.

4) **Decision making:** Most of us have worked in situations where decision making was easy—the choice was "whatever the boss says." But one reason that organizations try to encourage teamwork is so that people working on a process or problem have more say in decisions. Teamwork therefore comes with greater responsibility for everyone to actively participate in decision making. The skills and techniques you might find helpful include methods for determining how a decision should get made, which people or groups need to be included, what roles they should play (such as just contributing information or getting a vote in the final decision), how to develop criteria for selection between options, and so on.

Additional skills for effective teams

The collaboration skills discussed above are one aspect of getting people to work together as a team. But other skills are just as important. Have you ever been in teams or groups that didn't work very well? Sat in on meetings that seemed to never end? Gotten caught between people who would argue endlessly, making the same points over and over and over again?

Lean Six Sigma teams can't afford to waste time like that. Here are seven tips for avoiding those traps:

1. **Set goals.** As a team, discuss the project goals. Does everyone agree on what they mean? If not, resolve areas of disagreement or confusion.

2. **Assign accountability.** Whenever action is required, make sure that someone on the team is assigned the lead responsi-

bility to see that it is done. This applies to both ongoing tasks (such as arranging meeting times and locations) and project work (such as collecting data).

3. **Handle conflict.** The most effective teams reach a balance between openness and conflict. You *want* people to feel free to say what they think, because that's the only way you can be sure you're getting the best thinking from the team. But you *don't* want your team to spend its time in endless arguments. Finding this balance can take time, so be patient.

4. **Pay attention to how decisions are made.** Teams are brought together to make decisions about what needs to change in a process or product or service. So you will be judged largely on how effectively you reach *good* decisions. The skills needed to make good decisions include gathering data to explore options, documenting the reasons behind each decision, and involving every team member in the decision-making process.

5. **Make sure you have effective meetings.** A team gets most of its work done in meetings, so it's important that you use that time well. There are a lot of specific meeting skills and techniques that can help your team have good meetings. Team training courses usually cover topics like creating and using agendas, managing the meeting time, and so on.

6. **Foster continuous learning.** A goal of Lean Six Sigma teams is to constantly get better at everything they do—improving their work, making decisions, holding good meetings. That's why they emphasize continuous learning, always going over what they've done, identifying what went well and what didn't, and finding ways to get better the next time around.

7. **Collaborate with other groups.** Lean Six Sigma teams don't work in isolation. They are usually trying to improve procedures or a workplace where other people work. There may be other teams working on related areas. There are always people not on the team who have knowledge or skills the team could use. So learning how to work with other people and groups is another key to success. Your team will want to do things like

talking to customers to see what they want from your product or service. You'll want to talk to other people in the work area to see how their experience does or doesn't match your own. You'll also benefit from making connections with people who have done similar kinds of work.

Conclusion

It's easy enough to get a group of people and tell them to work together on a Lean Six Sigma project. But for them to be *effective* takes special team skills that most companies don't normally teach employees. If you have the chance to participate in team training, we advise that you jump at it! Skills like listening, brainstorming, and decision-making come in handy in any situation, not just when you're on a formal team.

CHAPTER 5

Key #4:
Base Decisions on Data and Facts

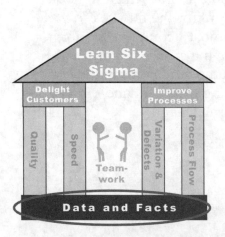

There are a lot of good reasons why data and facts form the true foundation of Lean Six Sigma. Want to know who your customers are and what they want? You need to collect data. Want to improve processes? You'll need to collect data on variation, defects, and process flow. Want to avoid the kind of needless arguments and squabbling that destroy teamwork? Have a rule that people must support their opinions with facts.

You also need data and facts because they'll save you a lot of trouble and prevent a lot of wasted dollars and time...

When the utilities in one state were de-regulated, one company suffered a great deal of "churn," losing customers about as fast as it gained new ones. They were forced to spend a lot more money on marketing now that they had to compete for customers.

The customer service staff had noticed several cases where new customers came on board then changed their minds right away, ultimately switching to a different company. Very quickly, these examples grew into a widely held assumption that *new* customer turnover was the reason behind the churn. The new customers were, the reasoning went, targets of marketing efforts by rival power suppliers.

The service staff therefore began focusing on how to keep these new customers from switching. They developed a new Welcome Pack explaining their services and benefits, which they began sending to thousands of new customers every week. At a cost of $8 a piece, this packet represented a significant investment.

At one point, however, a Lean Six Sigma team at this utility company collected data on churn. They found that new customers only accounted for about 4% of the total. The other 96% were *long-term* customers who were switching utility companies. In other words, the company was spending thousands of dollars each week on something that would solve only 4% of the problem! So they re-directed their marketing efforts to try to keep the customers they'd had for some time.

This company's experience is common. Their initial decision about what to do was wrong because they made it without data. Having data can make a huge difference in the decisions we make every day on the job, and is particularly important in improvement projects. Unfortunately, learning the data habit is harder than it has to be because of a number of roadblocks:

1) **A lack of available data.** Do you know how much work you have in your process at this very moment? Do you know how long, on average, it takes you to handle those work items, be they phone calls, requests, reports, bills, orders, etc.? Do you have a way to find out? Do you know what your work group's error rate is on average? How many of your customers are happy with the product or service you provide? How many are unsatisfied? Could *anyone* in your office answer questions about the quantity, quality, and speed of their work? For most people, the answers to those questions are "no" or "I don't know." People working on early Lean Six Sigma projects are often starting from scratch when they begin to collect data.

2) **Little training in collecting or analyzing data.** If you've never had to collect data before, the number of decisions involved will probably surprise you. What data should you collect?

How can you make sure it will answer the question your team is asking? How should you measure what it is you're trying to measure? How often should you take a measurement? How can you make sure that everyone collecting data will do it in the same way? Once you have the data, how can you analyze it to understand what it's telling you? There's a lot to learn!

3) **A historical pattern of using data only to punish or reward individuals, not to make decisions about improvement.** For many years, a lot of organizations have used data for only one purpose: to punish or reward people. Did you meet the sales quota? No? Then your pay will suffer. Did you finish all your customer calls in 60 seconds or less? Yes? Then you're a star. What's very different in Lean Six Sigma organizations is that data is used for *learning* and for *monitoring process performance*. You will be collecting data to understand what's going on in the process, where problems are arising, and what solutions will really work. Once improvements are made, you'll also be collecting data to track how well the process is doing, to detect any early signs of trouble, and to help you maintain the gains you've already made.

What kinds of data?

Once your company has made the commitment to collect data, the obvious question is "what kind of data?" Making that call is something you'll learn about if you go through training or participate on a team. To jump start your own thinking, we've given examples of actual data collected by teams in Chapters 7 and 8. In general, it all falls into two categories: **result measures** and **process measures:**

- Result measures reflect the *outcome* of a process or procedures—how the product or service turned out
- Process measures reflect what goes on to produce the result

In a baseball game, for example, the final score is a "result" measure. Stats like hits, errors, strikes, and walks are all "process" measures. They tell you what went on during the game to produce the final score.

You need both results and process measures to be effective in Lean Six Sigma. You absolutely *have* to keep track of the final result. But the only way you can improve a result is to change the process, and you'll need process measures to tell you what has to change and how.

What should you actually measure? Here are four typical types of data that teams find useful:

a. **Customer satisfaction** (a result measure): Data gathered through surveys or interviews on what customers think about your product or service, and what it's like doing business with your group or organization.

b. **Financial outcomes** (a result measure): What impact the quality and/or problems have on revenue, expenses, costs, etc.

c. **Speed/ lead time** (result or process measure): Data on how fast (or slow) your process is. "Lead time" is how long it takes for any individual work item to make it all the way from the beginning to the end of the process (when it is delivered to the customer). If measured at the end of the process, speed is a result measure. If measured on individual steps, it becomes a process measure. (You'll read more about speed and lead time in the next chapter.)

d. **Quality/defects** (result or process measure): How many errors are made, whether the product or service has flaws that affect the customer, and so on. Like speed, quality can be a result measure if the data are collected on the final product or service. But most teams also use it as a process measure, collecting data on what happens within the process.

Won't Gathering Data Slow Us Down?

At the end of its project, one team working on a purchasing problem realized that it had spent 75% of its project struggling to get good, reliable data. When some people hear a number like that, their first reaction is "we can't afford to spend that kind of time just gathering data!"

That kind of reaction is short sighted. It was BECAUSE of the time they invested in getting good data that the team in question could solve a problem that had been around for years. Getting the right data also allowed the rest of the project to go quickly. Whenever the team faced a decision such as "what solution should we try?" they could look at the data. So discussing the data replaced the kind of endless arguing that happens in teams who don't use data!

Skipping the data collection step is NOT an option in organizations that are really serious about Lean Six Sigma.

Conclusion

Roger Hirt, a Six Sigma specialist who works with the City of Fort Wayne, Indiana, was sitting in on a city panel meeting once where a city employee was reporting on an ongoing project. During the meeting, an influential member of the panel piped up to offer a solution. The employee thought about the suggestion and said, "I guess that would be possible." But then Roger stepped in. "Just a minute. We have to look at what the data tells us about the problem before we'd know whether that solution would do any good."

It's impossible to go back through history, or even look at organizations today, and see how many bad decisions were made because people didn't gather data. The number would be astronomical. Today, organizations that are using their resources most effectively insist on using data as often as they can.

But it's a hard habit to learn because we're so used to *not* collecting data. We have to re-train ourselves to pause before making a decision and think about whether there is existing data we could look at, or if we need to collect new data. Learning to ask one simple question—"What does the data tell us?"—will make a huge difference in your improvement efforts.

CHAPTER 6

Beyond the Basics
The Five Laws of Lean Six Sigma

If you've read Chapters 1 through 5 of this book, you've probably picked up on some key themes in Lean Six Sigma:

- Customers are important
- Speed, quality, and low cost are linked
- You need to eliminate variation and defects, and focus on process flow, if you want to deliver quality, speed, and low cost
- Data is critical to making sound business decisions
- People have to work together to make the kinds of improvements that customers will notice

This chapter takes these concepts one step further to introduce the Five Laws of Lean Six Sigma that describe simple principles we can use when selecting projects and making improvements. Before getting there, however, we need to first walk through a few more basic concepts and terms you'll need to know.

Some key terms

If you get involved in Lean Six Sigma efforts or hang around other people who are, you'll hear a number of words or terms that come up all the time. We'll walk through some of the most common.

WIP *(pronounced like the word "whip"—the letters stand for Work-in-Process)*

WIP is the amount of work that is officially in a process and isn't yet complete. That work can be anything from customer requests, checks waiting to be processed, phone calls you have to return, reports you need to complete, emails you need to respond to, a pile of incoming parts that need to be assembled, etc. Measuring or calculating WIP is as fundamental as having a doctor take your blood pressure at every visit. Like blood pressure readings, the amount of WIP is an overall indicator of process health.

Lead time and process speed

Lead time is how long it takes you to deliver your service or product once the order is triggered. Understanding what creates long lead time (meaning a slow process!) is much simpler than you might think, thanks to a simple equation known as **Little's Law** (named after the mathematician who proved it):

$$\text{Lead Time} = \frac{\text{Amount of Work-In-Process}}{\text{Average Completion Rate}}$$

We just covered Work-in-Process (WIP) above. Lead time is how long it takes for something to cycle through the process from start to finish. Completion rate is how many items of work get finished during any given time period (day, week, month).

Once you learn this equation, you can apply it quickly and easily to any process you work on. Most of us don't have a clue what our average delivery or lead time is, let alone what the variation is. But knowing these figures is critical in any Lean Six Sigma improvement effort. The thought of having to track an order through every step in the process is daunting, especially if you have a process that takes days or weeks to complete. (The city staff in Fort Wayne, Indiana, who issue building permits had a process that took 51 days on average. Can you imagine having to somehow track a single permit for almost two months?)

Little's Law isn't just a good theory. It has a lot of practical implications. For example, it tells us we can speed up any process by reducing the amount of WIP, even if we do nothing to speed up the completion rate. In other words, if we just eliminate WIP, we can get the work done faster without having to get better at actually doing the work. What a bargain!

Little's Law also allows us to estimate lead time simply by counting how much work is sitting around waiting to be completed (work-in-process) and how many "things" we can complete each day, week, etc.

Delays/queue time

Whenever you have WIP, you have work that is *waiting to be worked on*. In Lean Six Sigma, this work is said to be "in queue" (in line) and the time it sits around waiting is "queue time." Any time that work sits in queue is counted as a delay, no matter what the underlying cause. And delays are bad if you want to provide fast, timely service to customers.

Value-added and non-value-added work (waste)

Imagine that one of your customers came to tour your work area. What would they think of everything they saw? Every process has some work that *adds value in the eyes of your customers* (and hence is called **value-added** work). Each process also has work

that our customers would not want to pay for if they had the choice (the **non-value-added** work).

Another word for non-value-added work is **waste.** The goal of Lean Six Sigma is to eliminate as much waste as possible. Some waste we can never get rid of because no method known to humankind will make us 100% effective. But remember this: the more waste there is, the more delay you'll have in the process. Lean Six Sigma helps us recognize and eliminate waste and not simply accept it as "the way work is done around here."

Complexity

Many people would describe the processes they work in as "complex." But the word "complexity" has a special meaning in Lean Six Sigma. It refers to the number of different types of products, services, options, features, etc., that your processes have to handle. Some complexity is a good thing because it means your customers can get options that suit their needs. But too much complexity simply adds cost to the organization without any payback. Complexity issues mostly arise at a strategic level, such as which products or services a company should sell, what features they should offer, and so on. So you may hear the term from managers, but few Lean Six Sigma teams make decisions about complexity.

Process Efficiency

Since speed is a key goal of Lean, the natural questions are: How fast is fast? How slow is slow?

The answer comes by applying two concepts discussed above to calculate the **process cycle efficiency:** the ratio of **value-add time** (work that *customers* would recognize as necessary to create products or services they are about to purchase) to **total lead time** (how long the process takes from start to end). Process cycle efficiency lets us gauge the potential for cost reduction.

$$\text{Process Cycle Efficiency} = \frac{\text{Value-add Time}}{\text{Total Lead Time}}$$

Let's look at one example. A supplier for major auto companies knew that there was less than 3 hours of value-add time in their process. However, the total lead time from release of raw material into the line to shipment was an average of 12 days.

Based on having an 8-hour work day at the plant, the ratio of these two measures gives us process cycle efficiency:

Value Add Time = 3 Hours

Total Lead Time = 12 days X 8 hours/day= 96 Hours

Process Cycle Efficiency = 3 Hours/ 96 Hours = 3%

In other words, it was taking them 12 days to inject 3 hours of value into the product—the material is *waiting* for 11.6 days.

You may think that a 3% process cycle efficiency (PCE) is low, but it is fairly typical. A PCE of less than 10% indicates that the process has a lot of opportunity for improvement! And most processes today run at a cycle efficiency of less than 10%. (Take some data on your own processes and calculate the cycle efficiency. You'll be surprised.)

The laws of Lean Six Sigma

Now that you're getting the vocabulary down—customers, lead time, WIP, efficiency, complexity—you're ready for the Five Laws of Lean Six Sigma:

Law #1: The Law of the Market—Customer needs define quality and are the highest priority for improvement. You can't get sustained revenue growth without this.

Law #2: The Law of Flexibility—The speed of any process is proportional to its flexibility (that is, how easily people can switch between different types of tasks). If you want to be fast, you have to get rid of anything that causes a loss of productivity anytime people want to stop what they're doing and start on something new. (On the shop floor, inflexibility is seen in long set-up or changeover times. In service areas, inflexibility is seen when people have to track down missing information, change from one computer system to another, and so on.)

Law #3: The Law of Focus—Data shows that 20% of the activities in a process cause 80% of the problems and delay. So you'll make the most progress if you focus your efforts on those 20% (what you may hear some people call "Time Traps").

Law #4: The Law of Velocity (Little's Law)—The speed of any process is inversely related to the amount of WIP (work- or things-in-process). So as WIP goes up, speed goes down. As WIP goes down, a process speeds up. (Lesson: to make a process faster, cut down on how much work there is in process at any given time.)

Law #5: The Law of Complexity and Cost—The complexity of the service or product offering generally adds more costs and WIP than either poor quality (low Sigma) or slow speed (un-Lean) process problems. So one of your early improvement targets may well be reducing the numbers or varieties of products and services your work group is involved in. (This is a management decision that has to be based on good financial and market information.)

Conclusion

As you can probably tell from the past six chapters, implementing Lean Six Sigma requires time, effort, and dollars. So why would organizations go to all the trouble? Because the foundations of Lean Six Sigma we've discussed here have proven payback. Customers start getting better products and services, and become more loyal to your company and its brands. Costs go down. Employee loyalty goes up because people benefit from the Lean Six Sigma training and experience. In short, the company can be more profitable and provide better job security.

Just *how* all these changes come about is the subject of the next chapters. We'll show examples of how Lean Six Sigma is rolled out, examine how improvements get made, and look at what's in it for you to become involved.

PART 2

IMPLEMENTING LEAN SIX SIGMA

CHAPTER 7

When Companies Start Using Lean Six Sigma

Imagine that you are the CEO of a corporation with thousands of employees. Your executive team has decided that you need to invest in Lean Six Sigma if you want to become competitive. You want to launch a number of improvement projects so you can make a difference in the company's profits as quickly as possible. Unfortunately, only a few people in your company have any experience with Lean Six Sigma projects.

That means you have two big challenges: (1) picking projects you're sure will contribute to your corporate goals, and (2) training a large number of people so they can become effective team members. If you don't do these things, you'll never be sure that all the time your staff is about to put into the projects will be worthwhile.

How would *you* attack these challenges? In most companies, the solution combines:

- Creating new staff positions to shoulder most of the Lean Six Sigma responsibility
- Expanding the responsibilities of existing positions to include oversight of Lean Six Sigma efforts
- Developing appropriate training for anyone who will be involved in the Lean Six Sigma efforts
- Setting up new procedures to make sure the Lean Six Sigma efforts are linked to important business issues

Let's start by looking at what happens to staffing, then see what kind of training and procedures help support those staff.

Special staffing of Lean Six Sigma

Lean Six Sigma cannot be done well if everyone involved has other full-time jobs and responsibilities. So companies usually have some people who work on improvement efforts 100% of their time. But they also have to find ways to keep Lean Six Sigma tied into the "real" part of the company. And that's why they also add Lean Six Sigma responsibilities onto some existing positions.

The companies that invented Six Sigma back in the late 1980s developed special names for each of the new roles based on the practice in Karate of having different colored belts that indicate different levels of mastery.

The combination of these specialized "Belt" positions, as they are called, plus other staff involved in Lean Six Sigma is often called the Lean Six Sigma "infrastructure." Here again, each organization will have its own infrastructure, but let's look at seven typical roles and how they relate to Lean Six Sigma:

New positions created to staff Lean Six Sigma efforts

1) **Champions:** A Champion is an executive-level manager who has the responsibility for managing and guiding Lean Six Sigma efforts—and for making sure those efforts support and drive corporate priorities. Every organization should have a Champion reporting directly to the CEO or President. Large organizations may also have divisional or business unit Champions who report directly to the person in charge of that unit.

2) **Black Belts:** These are company employees who receive a minimum of 4 to 5 weeks of training on leadership and problem solving. They usually work full-time on Lean Six Sigma, though in some organizations they may only be part-time. They are responsible for leading or coaching project teams, and for delivering results on the selected projects.

3) **Master Black Belts:** These are Black Belts who have gone on to receive advanced training in more sophisticated problem-solving techniques. They also will have led a number of project teams and have a proven track record of delivering results. Their responsibilities include training and coaching Black Belts, monitoring team progress, and aiding teams as needed.

Staff who maintain their regular jobs but whose responsibilities expand to include Lean Six Sigma

4) **CEO & executives:** The Chief Executive Officer and other executives determine whether a company will adopt Lean Six Sigma. And they are ultimately responsible for setting corporate goals that will shape Lean Six Sigma priorities. They are also responsible for regularly monitoring and guiding how Lean Six Sigma resources are used.

5) **Business unit managers:** Every company is made up of different business units—departments, locations, plants, etc. In

some, the leaders of these business units are Presidents, in others, they are Vice Presidents. But no matter what the title, these Business Unit managers need to work closely with the Champion. Together, they use the unit's goals to define criteria for selecting projects. The final decisions about project targets belong to the Business Unit manager, because he or she will be accountable to the CEO for meeting annual goals.

6) **Line managers/process owners:** Line managers are the people who "own" the processes that will be improved by Lean Six Sigma. That is, they are responsible for authorizing changes in process procedures. (For that reason, some companies call these people Process Owners.) They are responsible for approving time for staff to attend training, serve on project teams, and so on. Support from line management is therefore critical to Lean Six Sigma success. When projects are launched in their work area, the line managers usually also serve as **project sponsors**. In that role, they are responsible for monitoring the team's progress, providing support as needed, and sustaining the business results delivered by the project team.

7) **Green Belts/Yellow Belts/White Belts/Team members:** These can be anyone in the organization who receives some level of awareness education or skill training in Lean Six Sigma. They usually maintain their regular jobs, but work part-time on projects in their work areas.

Typical training programs

Just like the Lean Six Sigma efforts themselves, training programs differ greatly from organization to organization. Typical levels of training include:

1) **An awareness course** *(White Belt training):* A brief course, often just a day or two long. The goal is to help people get familiar with Lean Six Sigma language and concepts. Project participation is usually *not* a requirement.

2) **An introductory methods/tools course** (*Yellow or Green Belt training*): The next level up is a course where people get to practice using the improvement methods and techniques. The training can last anywhere from one to two weeks. The Yellow Belt is intermediate between White and Green. The difference is that a Yellow Belt course is usually a bit shorter than Green Belt training, and people are required only to *participate* on projects. Most companies require people to *lead* projects to become a Green Belt.

3) **A skill-building tools/methods course** (*Black Belt training*): Black Belts are the core of the Lean Six Sigma support structure. In some companies they lead projects; in others, they serve as coaches and resources to several projects at a time. (See sidebar, below, for a description of a typical Black Belt course.)

4) **Advanced training in one or more specialties** (*Master Black Belt or enrichment courses*): There are a handful of sophisticated Lean and Six Sigma tools that are extremely valuable in some limited circumstances. It doesn't pay to train every Black Belt on them because they won't be needed as often as the more general Lean Six Sigma tools. Such skills are often covered either as part of Master Black Belt certification or in specialized enrichment classes available to Black Belts.

Black Belt Training

A well-rounded Black Belt training program is usually built around 4 to 6 weeks of classroom training, which includes one week of Leadership training. Typically, Black Belts attend a week of training, return to project work for a few weeks, come back for the second week of training, and so on.

- The course should cover Lean, Six Sigma, and complexity reduction methods, as well as project management skills and leadership.
- Each participant should get anywhere from 1 to 5 days of coaching from someone experienced in

making improvements and leading projects (such
as a Master Black Belt).

- Participants should have access to training materials, case studies, and other resources through both
printed and electronic means.

Linking Lean Six Sigma to business priorities

If you look at all the organizations that have adopted Six Sigma
or any of its predecessors—such as Total Quality Management—
you'll find a fair number that have invested a lot of time and
money with very poor results. If you look closely at these companies, you'll see problems such as…

1) Projects didn't address important business problems

2) The people working on Lean Six Sigma became "quality
commandos," looking down on anyone who wasn't
involved in improvement full-time

3) There was little or no monitoring of projects, so a lot of
teams spent a lot of time doing things that weren't
increasing profits or lowering costs

These problems are so common that Lean Six Sigma incorporates
ways to avoid them. Above all, Lean Six Sigma encourages the
mentality that improvement is something that should be done to
support business goals, not something done *instead* of the "real
work." In addition, there are two particular methods that are useful here:

- Developing a system for project selection
- Instituting a "tollgate" system for regular project evalua-
tion

Project Selection

If someone were to ask you what needs to be fixed or improved in your work area, odds are you could come up with a dozen different answers. Now multiply that by the number of people working for your department. And multiply *that* result by the number of different departments in your company—and you'll have an inkling of the kind of challenges that management faces in selecting projects. The problem isn't coming up with ideas. It's picking the *best* ideas from among the many possibilities. "Best" means projects that will have the biggest payoff (what your CEO would call "increasing shareholder value"), and that can be completed quickly with the resources available.

To solve this problem, Lean Six Sigma prescribes a process like that shown in Figure 7.1. The procedure starts with broad goals for the company as a whole (what executives may call "burning platforms"). Typical burning platforms include issues like "reach new customers," "reduce overhead costs," "speed up how quickly we get to market," and so on.

Figure 7.1—From Strategy to Execution

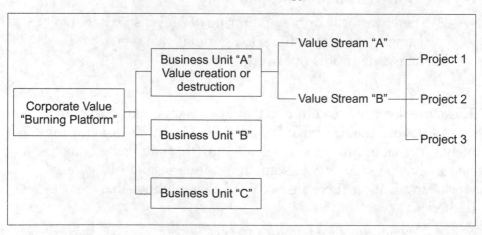

Those goals are translated down to business units, and then to specific processes (or "value streams") that will be targeted. Then the Champion and Black Belts will work with managers to identify specific projects to address the problems identified in the value stream.

The key to this sequence is maintaining the links at each step: making sure that business unit goals relate to corporate goals, and that project goals relate to the business unit goals. That way, projects will always be linked to corporate priorities. And *that* means managers are more likely to support them. It also means that Lean Six Sigma is more likely to be viewed as something to *help* managers and employees, rather than something that is stealing valuable resources away from the "real work."

A tollgate system for project review

In the past, teams were given their marching orders with little or no monitoring until the project was completed. Lean Six Sigma changes that. As you'll learn in the next chapter, most projects go through a standard sequence of activities known as Define-Measure-Analyze-Implement-Control or DMAIC (see the next chapter for details on DMAIC). In a Lean Six Sigma organization, managers review the project between each DMAIC phase, performing what is called a **tollgate** review. The purpose of these reviews is to…

- Update management on the team's progress
- Make sure the project is still critical to the organization
- Adjust or re-align the project as necessary
- Let management know what they can do to remove barriers for the team

Using this system helps make sure that the company's resources are used wisely, and that teams get the support they need to complete their projects on time and within budget.

Rollout of Lean Six Sigma

Launching Lean Six Sigma in a company involves a lot of different activities. Someone has to develop the needed training. Management needs to select the people to go through the training and the projects those people should work on. The timing and sequence of these activities varies from company to company. A typical process is shown in Figure 7.2 (next page). What's important in this picture is that...

- A lot happens within the first 100 days or so (because *slow* results aren't any better than *no* results in many cases!)

- Lean Six Sigma usually begins at the top levels of a company, with executive training and planning. (This is labeled as "initiation" in the chart.) It's important that executives get their training before others so that they can confidently lead Lean Six Sigma.

- There will usually be a formal announcement to the company either before or after executive training.

- Both project selection and training typically occurs in "waves." One group of people is chosen for training, then they begin work on the initial projects. Then another group is trained and starts project work, and so on.

Figure 7.2: Typical timeline for Lean Six Sigma rollout

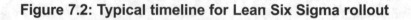

The timing of the waves varies a lot. Caterpillar, for instance, decided that it needed to have all its staff up to speed on Lean and Six Sigma methods very quickly. They trained 750 Black Belts in six months. Bank One, on the other hand, went through a year-long demonstration period of what it called "Focus 2.0" (their version of Lean Six Sigma). During this period, internal experts coached a *limited* number of teams on *major* projects. (There was no formal training except for on-the-spot coaching given by the experts.) The success of these projects created a lot of internal awareness of just what Lean and Six Sigma could do for the business, to the point where business units are now asking for training.

Conclusion

To have any chance of success, implementation of Lean Six Sigma must be accompanied by new positions, new training, and new ways for different layers of the organization to communicate. This new "infrastructure" helps companies translate their investment in Lean Six Sigma into measurable results to the organization and its customers.

CHAPTER 8

Making Improvements That Last
An Illustrated Guide to DMAIC and the Lean Six Sigma Toolkit

Every organization has problems that get "solved" over and over again, only to reappear. Teams work hard for months, generating solutions that people just *know* will work… but don't. This is another type of failure that Lean Six Sigma can't afford. That's why it uses a modern problem-solving method designed to avoid such problems. The model is called DMAIC (pronounced duh-MAY-ick), which stands for Define-Measure-Analyze-Improve-Control.

DMAIC has proven itself to be one of the most effective problem-solving methods ever used because it forces teams to use data to…

- Confirm the nature and extent of the problem
- Identify *true* causes of problems
- Find solutions that evidence shows are linked to the causes
- Establish procedures for maintaining the solutions even after the project is done

If you go through Lean Six Sigma training, you'll learn a lot about DMAIC and its data-based methods that are called "problem-solving tools." In this chapter of the book, we just want to introduce you to the logic of DMAIC and spotlight a few tools it uses to prevent the kinds of problems many teams used to run into. The next chapter will describe case studies where DMAIC was used to solve real problems.

Project chartering: The transition into Define

Before we get into the DMAIC process itself, you should be aware of what happens before a team gets started. Your management team will likely go through a project selection process to identify the projects they want to launch. The Champion (the corporate-level executive leading the Lean Six Sigma effort) will help your supervisor or manager draft a **project charter** to document what they want the team to accomplish. The charter is usually short—just a 1- to 2-page form. Some companies find it helpful to use a form similar to that shown in Figure 8.1.

Figure 8.1: Sample Project Charter

Project Charter

Proposal Process Improvement

Description: Improve quality proposal development by defining a precise process, managing to the process, improving efficiency, and reducing cycle time such that we can accomplish 15% more proposal work without increasing budgets.

Background: Engineering analysis needs to be done up front. Using analysis, develop a clear understanding of work scope. Educate senior management on proposal content. Prepare team to write/estimate based on a clearly defined technical scope of work.

In Scope: Product line proposals

Out of Scope: Highly efficient quality proposals

KPOV: Proposal cost

Goals:

1. 15% reduction of proposal cost based on metrics derived from previous large scale proposals
2. Increase proposal capacity by 10% (no increase in budget)
3. Reduce rework in the writing process

Assumptions:

1. Improving efficiency and reducing cycle time will result in the ability to do 15% more proposal work within the same budget
2. Full time dedicated proposal manager
3. Move rework resources into up-front planning and education to realize back end savings

Other Benefits:

1. Improve quality of written material
2. A standard proposal process will improve training, repeatability, and employee efficiency
3. A database / archive of material that can be reused for future proposals

Role	Name	Utilization	Start	End
Project Champion	Blanck, Mike	50%	8/20/2002	1/11/2003
Black Belt	Parra, Derek	100%	8/20/2002	1/11/2003
Financial Approver	Martin, Rick	10%	9/24/2002	1/11/2003
Team Member	Clark, Kathy	25%	8/20/2002	1/11/2003
Team Member	Robert, Rene	25%	8/20/2002	1/11/2003
Project Sponsor	Raney, Al	10%	8/20/2002	1/11/2003

A project charter captures the essence of a project. It describes what the team should accomplish, who will work on the project (and in what roles), timelines, and other key information.

What's important to know is that the charter you'll be handed if you serve on a team is just a draft. Your team will be expected to fine-tune it once you begin studying the problem in detail. In some cases, you may discover information that will make management re-think the decision to work on the project in the first place. Or the problem may be much bigger than they thought, and there's no way the team can tackle it. (So the team will have to work with management to agree on what some reasonable goals are.)

Teams should refer back to their charters throughout their projects. For one thing, this helps remind them about what they are supposed to do. It also gives them a chance to update the charter as they learn more information about the problem and its likely solutions.

A quick tour of DMAIC

The Define-Measure-Analyze-Improve-Control (DMAIC) process is usually described as a "structured, data-based problem-solving process." That means:

1) Doing specific activities in a specific sequence (that's the "structured" and "process" parts)

2) Gathering data in nearly every phase to help you make decisions (the "data-based" part)

3) Making sure that the solutions your team decides to use really will eliminate the cause of the problem you're trying to fix (the "problem-solving" part)

DEFINE-M-A-I-C

The purpose of this first stage of the DMAIC process is for a team and its sponsors to agree on what the project is. The kinds of things you'll do include...

- Discussing the project charter as a team.
- Getting customer data.

- Reviewing existing data about the process or problem.

- Drafting a high-level map of the process. ("Process maps" are one type of improvement tool used often in DMAIC. Here in Define, they are used to help establish the project boundaries.)

- Setting up a plan and guidelines for your team.

Why should you do these things? They help you...

- **Develop a *shared* understanding of the business priorities for your project.** (That word "shared" is key. Many teams get bogged down when people argue over what kind of data the team should collect or what solutions are best. That happens a lot when people don't realize they have different ideas about what the team should be doing.)

- **Confirm the opportunity.** Talk to customers and look at any existing evidence to confirm that the problem that management wants you to solve is a real opportunity. This work will help you refine the project goals. In rare cases, a project may get canceled if the data does not support further work.

- **Reach agreement with management on a *realistic* scope for the project.** If your team thinks the project is too big (or too small), you need to negotiate with management to change the scope, add resources, and/or extend the deadline as appropriate.

- **Agree on how "success" will be measured.** A common mistake in the past was for teams and sponsors to NOT define upfront how they would know if the project is successful. A team would see the number of mistakes dropping, but what the manager wanted was an increase in sales. A team needs to know what its sponsor will be looking at to judge whether they are successful.

- **Set the team up for success.** Sometimes, a project team consists of people who work together every day. Other times, it brings together people from different departments who don't know each other at all. The early work in Define will help team members get comfortable working together in an improvement setting.

Example Define tool #1: the SIPOC diagram
(high level process map)

A core principle of Lean Six Sigma is that defects can relate to anything that makes a customer unhappy—long lead time, variation in lead time, poor quality, or high cost, for instance. To address any of these problems, the first step is to take a process view of how your company goes about satisfying a particular customer requirement. The tool for creating a high-level map of the process is called SIPOC, which stands for:

Suppliers: the individuals or groups who provide whatever is worked on in the process (information, forms, material)

Input: the information or material provided

Process: the steps used to do the work

Output: the product, service, or information being sent to the customer

Customers: the next step in the process, or the final (external) customers

An example of a SIPOC diagram is shown in Figure 8.2. A project team in a company that leased equipment was asked to reduce the number of errors in orders and corresponding invoices. As a first step, they created the SIPOC diagram to identify the basic elements of the process they were supposed to study.

Figure 8.2: SIPOC process diagram

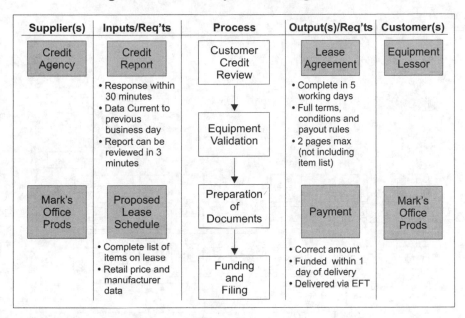

This figure shows a SIPOC diagram for an organization that leases equipment. As you can see, it not only shows all the SIPOC elements, but also critical-to-quality (CTQ) indicators (such as "complete in 5 working days").

Example Define tool #2: Value Stream Map

SIPOC diagrams present a very simple view of a process, and are very useful for visually representing the basic elements of a process under study. But they don't really help a team understand what needs to be changed in a process. For that, you need more detailed process maps (also called "flowcharts").

One type of process map used frequently in Lean Six Sigma projects is called a value stream map. These maps not only show the process flow, but also display actual process data. (See example in Figure 8.3, top of next page). Because they include data, value stream maps can help teams pick out specific points in the process that have problems such as long wait times or lots of errors.

Figure 8.3: Value Stream Map

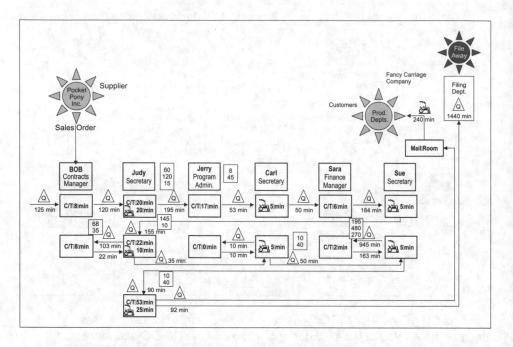

This value stream map, based on an actual process, captures the main sequence of activities in the boxes across the top line. The triangles and other notations show wait times (delays) and rework loops (another form of waste). Notice that the order begins by waiting 125 minutes "in queue" at Bob's activity before he spends 8 minutes adding value. Then it waits 120 minutes at Judy's station before she adds 20 minutes of value, etc. The order makes several loops back and forth among Judy, Bob, and Sue. Creating a map like this highlights wasted time and effort that usu- ally isn't apparent to people mired in the process. Why the long queue times? Because there is a lot of work-in-process that has to be handled before any new item of work can be handled.

D-**MEASURE**-A-I-C

Measure is the heart of what makes Lean Six Sigma work when other approaches haven't. If you don't gather data, you'll likely end up with a lot of quick-hit projects with short-lived or disappointing results. Combining data with knowledge and experience is what separates true improvement from just tinkering with a process. In Measure you will...

- Evaluate the existing measurement system
  - Improving it if necessary
  - Developing a measurement system if you don't already have one
- Observe the process
- Gather data
- Map the process in more depth

Actions like these are necessary so you can...

- **TRUST your data.** You'd be surprised at how often a team spends a lot of time collecting data only to find out that their measurement system is unreliable. They discover that people were "starting the clock" at different points in the process when trying to measure cycle time. Or that people were reading an instrument gauge differently. Or had different definitions of what a "defect" was. If you're going to be basing your decisions on data, you have to make sure you can trust what the data are telling you.

- **Base decisions on facts and reality.** We've said this several times in the book already: DMAIC is a data-based method. People's opinions still count, but everything must be checked against what the data is telling you.

- **Document what's REALLY going on in the process.** Kevin Fast, a Lean Six Sigma Black Belt and Manager of Quality Initiatives for Lifetime Support at Lockheed Martin in Moorestown, New Jersey, made an interesting observation: "When a project team comes together to define their process," he remarked, "someone will say, 'You do *that*? I didn't know you did that!' Or 'You do this? I do this, too.' It's just amazing how people who have worked on a process for a long, long time often don't realize everything that goes on." Kevin was right. That's why a Lean Six Sigma team has to *document* what is really going on.

- **Understand what's important to improve.** Here's a tip that will make your task as a "process improver" much easier. *Of all the dozens or hundreds of actions you and your coworkers perform in your process, only a few of them make a real difference to your customer.* Your job will be to find and improve those key tasks… then eliminate as much of the "non-value-adding" work as possible.

Example Measure tool #1: process observation

We've already talked about the need to document or "map" a process. But before you even get to that point, what you need to do is simply go out and watch what's going on. In the famous words of Yogi Berra, "You can observe a lot just by watching." There simply is no substitute for impartial observation as a way to confirm what really happens in a process and identify waste and inefficiencies that are built into how work is currently done.

Example Measure tool #2: time value map

A Time Value Map looks at how time is spent in a process. The chart consists of a timeline with bars broken out to highlight work that adds value in your customers' eyes and work that doesn't. One example is shown in the Figure 8.4 on the next page.

Example Measure tool #3: Pareto charts

One of the reasons why many improvement efforts have failed in the past is that people make *general* changes targeted at *general* problems. What's different in DMAIC is that you use data to pinpoint a *specific* cause of the problem. Then you develop solutions for that specific cause.

One of the most common tools used to help focus a team's efforts is a type of bar chart called a Pareto chart (pronounced "puh-RAY-toe"—it's named after an Italian economist). In a

Figure 8.4: Time Value Map

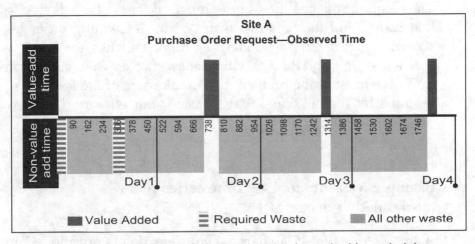

On a Time Value Map, the work that adds value is marked by a dark bar above the timeline. All the rest of the time is waste. In this case, there is some work that doesn't help customers (and, in that sense, is non-value-add) but that is required for accounting or tracking purposes. That's the "required waste" time shaded by stripes.

Figure 8.5: Pareto Chart

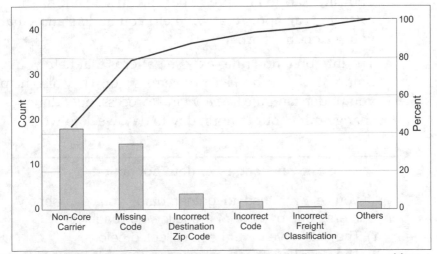

Pareto charts help focus a team on the biggest contributors to a problem. This chart shows how often different types of billing errors occurred. The team should focus its efforts on the first two types of errors, since solving those would reduce the number of defects by 80%.

Pareto chart, each bar represents a different element of a problem. The height of the bar shows how much of the problem is due to that cause, and the bars are arranged in descending order (as shown in Figure 8.5, previous page). Almost always, the first few bars will be tall, and the rest will be *much* shorter. That means you can solve most of the problem if you take care of the issues represented by the tall bars—that is, *focus* your efforts on the few biggest causes.

Example Measure tool #4: time series plots
(also called "run charts")

A time series plot is a chart where data points are plotted in sequence along a timeline (see Figure 8.6). Time plots are an important DMAIC tool for several reasons:

- They are very easy to construct. Once you learn a few basics, you can create one quickly with pencil and paper (useful even in this computer age!), or easily enter the needed data into a software program.

- They are easy to interpret. There are just a handful of rules you can apply that will help you understand what you see on the chart.

- The interpretation rules expose patterns that help you pinpoint *when* and *where* problems occur. They also help you understand the *variation* in a process, how things change from hour to hour, day to day, week to week.

The challenges of data collection

If you've ever tried to gather data, you've probably encountered one or more of the following roadblocks:
1) The data have never been collected before
2) The data have been collected, but for all practical purposes are unavailable (lost in a file cabinet, stuck in an obscure software program, etc.)
3) There is so much data that it's difficult to figure out

Figure 8.6: Time Series Plot

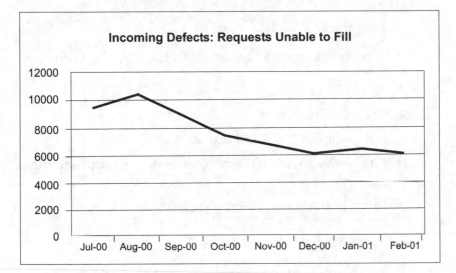

This chart was used during a project to track progress. Even without knowing any statistics or doing any complicated calculations, you can tell from this time series plot that the number of defects dropped substantially as the team made improvements.

what has priority or what is most meaningful

4) The data does not really measure what you think it measures

If any of these conditions hold true for your team, expect to spend a lot of time deciding what data to collect and finding a way to collect it.

D-M-**ANALYZE**-I-C

The purpose of the Analyze phase is to make sense of all the information and data collected in Measure, and to use that data to confirm the source of delays, waste, and poor quality. A challenge that all teams face in Analyze is *sticking to the data*, and not just using their own experience and opinions to reach conclusions about the root causes of problems. The things you'll do include…

- Looking for patterns in the data
- Targeting places where there's a lot of wasted time

These actions will allow you to…

- Find clues to the REAL causes
- Find ways to make the process faster without sacrificing quality
- Identify the most critical process factors to control

Example Analyze tool #1: cause-and-effect diagrams

A cause-and-effect diagram is a "thinking" tool that helps a team organize the ideas they have about potential causes of a problem. Organizing ideas this way serves two purposes:

1) It helps a team make sure they haven't overlooked potential causes
2) It helps a team decide which causes to investigate further

A cause-and-effect diagram is sometimes called a **fishbone** because it resembles the skeleton of a fish. As you can see in the example on the next page (Figure 8.7), the team's problem statement is named in the "head" of the fish, with potential causes arranged in sets of "bones" linked to the head. The smallest bones are the most specific types of causes that contribute to the next larger level of bone, and so on.

Cause-and-effect diagrams do not tell you *which* of the potential causes is the culprit. They are just a good way for the team to document which theories it has considered, which have been targeted for further investigation, and, ultimately, which have been verified.

Figure 8.7: Example cause-and-effect diagram

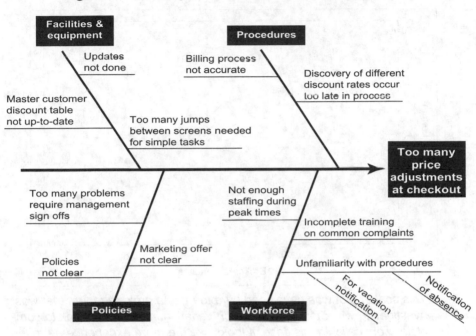

This team used a cause-and-effect diagram to make sure they had identified a wide range of reasons why clerks need to make so many price adjustments when customers check out. The team then selected the ones they thought were most likely, and gathered data to see if their ideas were right.

Example Analyze tool #2: scatter plots

The **scatter plot** is a simple tool that can help determine if a relationship exists between two measures or indicators. The example shown in Flgure 8.8 (top of next page) was created to explore whether broker experience affected how long it took to complete client calls. The downward slope of the line shows that more-experienced brokers are able to complete calls more quickly.

If customer satisfaction was high with the shorter calls, the team would then have to see what the experienced brokers knew that let them get done faster, and transfer that knowledge to less-experienced brokers.

Figure 8.8: Scatter Plot

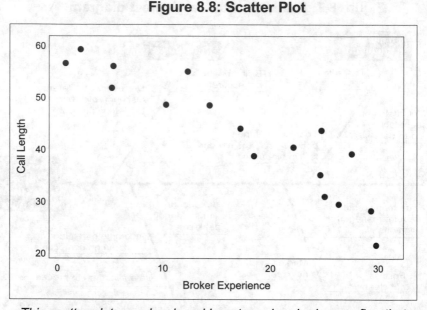

This scatter plot was developed by a team in a brokerage firm that was investigating why there was so much variation in the time it took to complete client calls. In this case, it looks like the more experience a broker has, the quicker he or she can complete the calls.

Scatter plots provide a powerful visual image of how potential process factors are (or are not) related to a key outcome. Often, the visual impression is enough to confirm (or rule out) a specific course of action. If necessary, more advanced statistical tools can be used to quantify the degree of relationship between the two factors.

D-M-A-**IMPROVE**-C

The sole purpose of Improve is to make changes in a process that will eliminate the defects, waste, costs, etc., that are linked to the customer need identified in the Define stage. The links in the last sentence are critical. The team must make sure that the causes they're looking at in Improve affect the problem or need defined in its charter. The changes they make must affect the causes they confirmed in Analyze. The things you'll do include…

- Using creativity exercises to identify a range of possible solutions (rather than rely on things that are tried-and-true)
- Reviewing existing Best Practices (documented procedures known to produce good results) to see if any can be adapted to your situation
- Developing criteria for selecting solutions
- Piloting the chosen solution
- Planning for full-scale implementation

What does this get you? It will help your team…

- *Not* get stuck with the same old solutions that don't work
- Develop new solutions that you KNOW are linked to the REAL causes
- Justify/explain why one solution was chosen over another
- Learn about what will and won't work in reality

Example Improve tool #1: PICK chart (evaluating solution alternatives)

There comes a time in every project where the team has developed a number of alternative solutions they think could improve the problem. There are several ways that they can compare those alternatives. One of the simplest to construct is the **PICK chart** (Figure 8.9, top of next page). On this type of chart, your team just needs to identify how much effort it will take to implement your solution ideas, and what kind of payoff you expect. Performing this analysis helps you decide which ideas you should implement for sure, which may need more work, and which ones you should just abandon.

Figure 8.9: PICK Chart

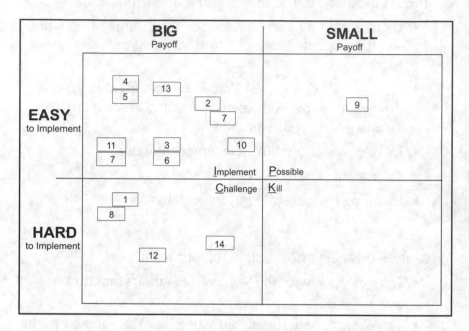

*A PICK chart helps a team organize and prioritize its solution ideas
by separating them into four categories: Possible, Implement, Challenge,
or Kill. Here, most of the solution ideas were easy to implement
and would have a big payoff—they fell into the Implement quadrant.
Four ideas would have a big payoff but were harder to implement,
so the team needed to Challenge these ideas (was the payoff really
that big? were there easier ways to accomplish the same effect?).
Only one idea had a small payoff, and therefore was considered
Possible; no ideas fell into the automatic Kill category.*

Example Improve tool #2: Four-Step Rapid Setup

A manager who wants to prepare a monthly report
starts gathering together the information he needs. He
realizes that this month's sales figures aren't broken out by
region, so he calls over to accounting and tells them to
email the regional split as quickly as they can. He also
discovers that he has updates on only three of the four

Lean Six Sigma projects in his unit. So he spends about 20 minutes tracking down a Black Belt and getting a verbal update on the fourth project. Then all he has to do is get the month's wages/benefits figures from HR, and he's ready to work on the report.

# # #

Dave, one of the more experienced technicians in IT knows more about PCs than nearly anyone else in the company. Trouble is, the graphic design group is on Macintoshes. So even though Dave spends 95% or more of his time supporting the PC users, he still has to answer a handful of calls each month from the Mac users. He describes the experience as having to "reconfigure" his brain so he can switch from thinking in Microsoft Windows to thinking in Apple's OS X.

# # #

The people who work on the old machinery down in the steel plant dread the days when they have to process a number of different grades of steel. Changing steel grade means adjusting the machines. Minimally, they lose about a half hour each time they have a changeover. And that's if everything goes right, which it doesn't always. That's why most of the time they produce a lot of one grade of steel at a time, even if no customers need it.

Odds are that at least one of these examples reflects what happens in your job—needing to track down information to finish a task, switching from one set of tasks to another, doing work in large "batches" because it seems easier, having some element of your job that you only rarely perform. Can you tell what they all have in common?

The answer is that all of these processes have problems that divert people away from their "value-add" work. If they could have the information at their fingertips, if it was easier to switch from one computer system or grade of steel to another, these people could get a lot more work done. Problems like these slow down a process.

In Lean terminology, the situations described above are all considered **setup problems** that delay or interrupt people as they try to complete the "value-add work." The Lean tool for attacking setup time is the Four-Step Rapid Setup method. The actual procedures are too detailed to go into in this book. Very briefly, the four steps cover techniques like doing prep work in parallel with value-add work, eliminating the need for set up work, and so on. In short, the principle of this method is to **eliminate anything that interrupts or hinders productivity.**

Here's an example from a service situation (the principles hold true for manufacturing as well). The buyers in one division of Lockheed Martin had to purchase parts for 14 different business units—each of which had its own computer system. To process the purchase orders, a buyer would log onto one unit's system, work through all of its purchase requests, log off that system and onto another unit's system, and so on. Switching from one system to another could take the buyers as much as 20 minutes at a time—which is why they would do all the orders from one unit before going on to the next.

Because of the large number of purchase requests, it could take a buyer a full day to complete the orders for one unit. With 14 units, that meant each unit's orders would be handled only once every three weeks! Is it any wonder that the units complained about how long it took them to receive the materials they wanted?

The Four Step Rapid Setup method challenges people to think about work like "switching computer systems" in new ways. Can it be eliminated? If not, what can be done to make it simpler and shorter?

In this case, the answer was that yes, it could be eliminated. The team worked with the technology department to develop a system where all the orders from all the sites were automatically downloaded into a central database every day. So the buyers just had to log into one database to see all the orders from all the units. They could also tell which requests were high priority and process those first.

Most likely you won't have heard of the Four Step Rapid Setup method before. So why did we take so much time talking about it? For two reasons: At a general level, we wanted to show that the Lean Six Sigma toolkit includes tools that help you develop solutions as well as tools for gathering and understanding data. More specifically, the Four Step method is often THE critical tool for accelerating process speed. In the Lockheed Martin example discussed above, for example, the average time it took for buyers to enter orders went from 14 or more days on average to 1 or 2 days.

D-M-A-I-CONTROL

The purpose of Control is to make sure that any gains your team makes will last. That means creating procedures and work aids that will help people do their jobs differently from now on. The team must transfer what they learned to the process owner and ensure that everyone working on the process is trained in using the new, documented procedures. In Control you will...

- Document the new, improved procedures
- Train everyone
- Set up procedures for tracking key "vital signs"
- Hand-off ongoing management to the process owner
- Complete the project documentation

The actions will help you...

- **Prevent backsliding.** Changing habits is a lot harder than changing the switches on a machine. The actions listed above will make it easier for people to use the new procedures and NOT slip back into the old way of doing things.

- **React quickly to future problems.** Tracking the vital signs for your process will help you respond quickly when and if new problems appear. The sooner you react, the more likely you are to be able to find the cause and put a new solution in place.

- **Share the learning with others in your organization.** Chances are there are other people in your organization doing the same kind of work that you do, or at least something very similar.

Having your team's work documented in a simple way will help other people share the learning and insights from your team.

Example Control tool #1: control charts

Probably the most common tool in Control is a control chart, which you can think of as a super-charged time series plot. Like a time plot, the data points are plotted in time order. But control charts have additional lines on them (**control limits**) that are used for interpreting patterns in the data. (See example in Figure 8.10.) Basically, if any points go outside the control limits, that's a signal of unusual variation. Someone should investigate what's going on in the process right away. (In addition, specific patterns of points within the limits are also used as signals.)

Control charts look complicated, but they are fairly easy to construct based on some simple mathematical formulas. Team members will often get help from a Black Belt and/or statistical software for constructing these charts.

Figure 8.10: Control Chart

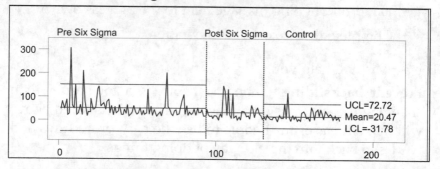

Like a time series plot, a control chart starts by charting the data in the order in which they are collected. The points hover around a center line, drawn at the mean (= average). The two outer lines—one above and one below the mean—are called "control limits." The distance between the control limits indicates how much variation can be expected in the process. Points that go outside the limits are signals that something odd or unusual is happening that the team needs to investigate. (There are several signals seen on this chart.) This team saw the amount of variation drop dramatically from before to after the project—just look at how much *closer the control limits are in the "control" phase compared to the "pre-six-sigma" phase. As we learned in Chapter 3, reducing variation is a good thing.*

Conclusion

It takes discipline to find real solutions to problems. The DMAIC framework provides that discipline and structure to teams. It can sometimes seem tedious to work through all the steps of Measure and Analyze—gathering data, learning lessons, realizing you have to gather even more data. Perhaps the biggest challenge you'll face is the temptation to skip all the messy stuff in the middle and go right from defining the problem to implementing solutions.

If you work on a DMAIC project, we promise that you'll have periods where you think it isn't worth it. When that happens, keep in mind that DMAIC wasn't developed by people who had nothing better to do with their time. It's the result of years of experience from people who've learned the hard way what it takes to make improvements that last.

CHAPTER 9

The Experience of Making Improvements

What It's Like to Work on Lean Six Sigma Projects

When Heather Presley was asked to participate in Green Belt training at the City of the Fort Wayne, Indiana, she'd been with the city for about 7 years. She'd started out as a customer service representative in the Utility department, then moved into a division of the Economic Development department—the people responsible in part for attracting new business to the city. She'd also recently finished getting her bachelor's degree, where she had heard about something called "Six Sigma," but didn't really know what it meant.

A new mayor, Graham Richard, had just been elected in Fort Wayne. He was an entrepreneur and former state representative who had extensive training in Six Sigma himself. When first elected, he made it a point to visit every city department and describe his vision of Fort Wayne and its government. Part of that vision included using Six Sigma to provide better services to citizens and improve the efficiency of city operations. "That's where I started to get excited about this idea of change that was happening," says Heather.

When Heather's boss asked her to take the city's new Green Belt course, she agreed. "In Fort Wayne, this training consists of one full day each week for 10 weeks," says Heather. "In between, I was expected to work on a project as well as do my regular job."

Picking a project wasn't hard for Heather. She already had one in mind. "In Economic Development, we were like customer service agents to business," explains Heather. "If they needed help finding a building, or getting a business started, we would direct them in the proper venue to get that done."

The problem was that the city's permit process for contractors was truly awful. "Businesses would tell us, 'I'll never build inside city limits again. Your permit process is so horrible, I don't want to go through it anymore. It's demeaning.' It got so bad, I used to call myself 'complaint central.'"

Then one day, the president of the building contractors association called Heather. "That's where the project idea came from," she says, "in talking with my customers."

Even before Heather began her project, the mayor had commissioned a Red Tape committee to address the problem. The permit process involved 15 departments, and the committee included representatives from each department. Heather knew it wouldn't be easy to work with that many departments, but she realized how important it was to the city to improve the permit process.

Launching the project

When the project was formally launched, Heather had a core team of people who met regularly but were not directly involved in the process. "We were the analysts, the data collection experts," says Heather. She also began working with the various departments. "I had to pull together people in small groups. Some people were 'experts' on the process. Others were what we call 'internal customers,' the departments that use some of the 'products' of the permit process."

When the project began in the spring of 2001, one of the first steps Heather took was to map out the process. "I worked with the Planning department, because they were the agency that collected and distributed all the paperwork. Then I took that map to other departments to see if they agreed. And I'd find differences."

What was interesting, says Heather, is that people she thought of as "experts" knew how the process *should* work. Then she'd talk to the managers in the departments to find how the process *could* work. And she'd get yet another view by talking to frontline staff and finding out how the process actually *did* work! "I had to talk to the managers separately from the frontline folks to get the truth on both sides—what it should be and what it really is. That way I could eliminate some of the politics and begin to find ways to bridge the gap."

The actions

Heather found that some of the tools she learned in her Green Belt training were very helpful in finding solutions to the permit process problems. "We used tools like a cause-and-effect matrix and Failure Modes and Effects Analysis, or FMEA. Both of these tools help you look at what can go wrong with a process so you can find ways to fix it," she explains. In fact, she adds, the Green Belt training doesn't go into the more complex Lean Six Sigma tools. "The projects are supposed to be simple enough that you can get through it with just those basic tools," says Heather.

One of the main lessons Heather learned is that the process hadn't been documented before, so no one really knew how it should (or could) work. Once some of the kinks were worked out, Heather realized she needed to make it easier for people from all the various departments to track what was going on in the process. "What I ended up doing was using the information I collected through the project to create a simple software program to track the permits. The city Champion got the computer folks to get it on the main computer servers, so anybody could access it."

The result?

Heather was later promoted to Community Development Projects Administrator in the Division of Community Development, but before she left the permit process behind she could see signs of progress already.

Originally, the turnaround time on processing contractor permits had been 61 days on average, with a few of them taking up to 180 days (nearly six months!). Heather's team had identified a number of changes by August of 2001, which got fully implemented in September and October. Those changes had a dramatic effect. "By December of 2001, we were turning around 75% of the permits in 30 days or less," she says. "And we kept making improvements. By April of 2002, the average was just under 12 days.

"I also started getting feedback from the developers and other people in the departments saying they were getting a better feeling about the process. We had one big customer that had submitted more than 300 permits over the past 20 years. Only one of those 300 had been signed off in 1 day. Now, 1-day sign offs are routine. So they are really happy about that!" says Heather.

The Benefit of Champion Support

As you may recall from Chapter 7, most organizations using Six Sigma designate a corporate Champion, a high-ranking executive who is responsible for the overall effort. These Champions often play a big role in helping individuals succeed with their projects.

"The Champion of my project was a guy named Andy Downs. He headed up the Red Tape committee and was the Mayor's Chief of Staff," says Heather. "He handled some of the roughest times for me single-handedly. With him breaking down all the barriers, like a Champion should, I was able to get done what I needed to get done and not get bogged down. Without a good Champion, this project never would have worked."

Is Heather's experience typical?

Every organization will have its own way of making improvements. But several aspects of Heather's experience are typical of what you may experience:

- The problem chosen for improvement was critical to the organization.

- She worked mostly with a small core team, pulling in other experts and going into the other departments as needed.

- Because the process had never been studied before, she was able to make a lot of progress with basic Lean Six Sigma tools like process mapping.

In other respects, this project is different from what you might expect:

- **Big problems like these are usually worked on by more experienced Belts.** Most companies would not assign a new Green Belt to work on such a big, complex problem, especially one that involved 15 departments! Typically, a more experienced Black Belt would be assigned to lead the project. Or a company might wait until more people had Lean Six Sigma training before tackling a project like this.

- **Many companies will push for faster results.** Because Heather and her team were new to improvement and only working on the project part-time, it took five months before they could start making the process changes. Companies who want to make faster progress will most likely have one or more Black Belts work on the project full-time, involving other staff as needed.

- **In many organizations, all team members will receive some level of training.** This building permit process was one of the first done in the city, and few people had had any training at that point. Many companies will do more widespread Green (or White or Yellow) Belt training, and use the participants to staff project teams.

Conclusion

Teams go through a lot of highs and lows doing project work. There's the excitement of meeting customers, probably for the first time. There's the frustration of realizing that the kind of data you need just to assess current performance doesn't exist. There's the reward that comes from making changes in a process that actually makes life better for you and your coworkers.

We can't predict exactly what kind of experience you'll have if you participate on a project team. But we can guarantee that it will be a valuable learning experience. The skills and tools you learn in making improvements can be easily transferred to helping you improve your everyday work.

CHAPTER 10

Six Things Managers Must Do
How to Support Lean Six Sigma

The preceding chapters of this book are intended to help employees fill their role in supporting your Lean Six Sigma initiative. But as we all know *their* success depends on the environment that managers create around that initiative. There are six "must do's" for managers that will set the stage for employee success:

1. Pick the right projects
2. Pick the right people
3. Follow the method
4. Clearly define roles and responsibilities
5. Communicate, communicate, communicate
6. Support education and training

1. Pick the right projects

One of the reasons that previous quality improvement methods have failed is that people had no guidelines to work from in selecting projects. So employees would end up doing projects like "redesign the cafeteria" or "set up a new system for assigning parking spaces." Yes, these kinds of projects may make some people feel better, but even if they were successful, the company's customers saw no gains in quality, speed, or cost. And managers saw only money going out with no benefit to the numbers that the CEO was watching! No wonder that a lot of them became disillusioned and stopped supporting the improvement efforts.

The early days of Six Sigma weren't much different. Often times, a company would let the Black Belts pick projects, sometimes with input from Champions and process owners. Unfortunately, this approach often led to projects that might generate improvements, but that weren't really linked to critical business needs.

The companies who have contributed to the development of Lean Six Sigma know that it lives and dies with project selection. If you don't have people working on the right things, it won't matter how good they get at problem solving and improvement. So there's a lot more guidance given to people now in selecting the "right" projects, those that...

- **Are linked to corporate strategies and priorities.** There should be clear links all the way down from your CEO's annual strategies to specific projects. (This presumes that corporate strategies have been chosen to benefit your customers as well as the business, so that the frontline projects can also be traced directly to benefits that your customers will notice.)

- **Are realistic in scope.** Far too many companies have seen quality initiatives fail because they were picking problems of the "solve world hunger" scope. In some cases, it does pay to have an experienced team of problem solvers attack broad, complex problems. But by and large you'll be better off selecting projects you think that new project teams can realistically complete in three months or less. How will you know? You may not, at first. But you can talk to other people involved with project teams and learn from their mistakes. You can learn-as-you-go, periodically evaluating projects launched in your organization to learn what makes for a realistic project in your environment.

- **Have identifiable and measurable hard results.** Lean Six Sigma puts a strong emphasis on making sure that the dollars you invest in projects can be measured on the bottom line. There are some up front costs: a lot of time and expense occurs during the training and startup phase. But a well-designed Lean Six Sigma process more than pays for its costs during the first year of implementation. (That said, don't ignore the softer results you'll see with projects, such as improved morale, fewer hassles in the workplace, greater collaboration, and so on. It's just that rarely, if ever, should you pick a project solely because of its soft-side potential.)

A final tip on project selection: keep the project pipeline well stocked. Typically, companies go through a formal project discovery or identification process each year, then narrow down the list based on capabilities and priorities. In doing so, you need to think about not only what projects you're going to launch immediately, but what projects will come *next*. When one project is completed, what will take its place? Suppose, for example, that a team discovered that a project really isn't as important to customers as originally thought, or that the expected return isn't as large as predicted. What would you have the team do instead?

Focus + Prioritization = Fast Results

One of the main selling points of Lean Six Sigma is that companies who do it well get really quick payback from their investment of time and effort. That happens because they use the guidelines discussed here to select IMPORTANT projects that are linked to the key issues for the business. In the past, an organization might launch 50 projects at a time just because they all sounded like good ideas. But Lean Six Sigma organizations are more likely to focus attention on the 5 or 10 that they can show have the biggest potential.

Someone Who Needs Help With Project Selection

2. Pick the right people

A big theme in this book has been adding rigor to decisions that previously have been based on judgment, experience, or gut instinct alone. That theme holds true when selecting the people to fill the new Lean Six Sigma roles we defined back in Chapter 7 (Champions, Black Belts, project team members, etc.). Going into details is beyond the scope of this book, but be aware that a lot of people have spent a lot of time developing methods that can help you identify the individuals or groups (and the combination of skills, abilities, personalities) to fill the new positions.

3. Follow the method

The vast majority of methods and techniques associated with Lean Six Sigma have evolved over the past few decades (or longer). They are based on a lot of experience with what does and doesn't work in practice. You can be a more effective manager if you adopt Lean Six Sigma practices such as...

- Always asking to see the data when employees present you with a suggestion or idea.
- Working with a Black Belt to develop ways to "make waste visible" in your work area. Simple data charts and flow charts, maintained by you or your employees, can keep people focused on improvement goals.
- Fully participating in the DMAIC reviews for teams working on issues that affect your work area.

4. Clearly define roles and responsibilities

In setting up a Lean Six Sigma infrastructure, you also set up potential conflicts in authority and responsibility. Being clear about the responsibilities of both the management and Lean Six Sigma roles will help you avoid innumerable conflicts.

A **RACI** format that helps people sort out and clarify responsibilities is a useful tool for this situation. The letters stand for different levels of expectation:

- **Responsibility**, for people who are expected to actively participate in the activity and contribute to the best of their abilities
- **Accountability**, denoting the person ultimately held responsible for the results
- **Consultation**, for the people/groups who either have a particular expertise they can contribute to specific decisions (i.e., their advice will be sought) or who must be consulted with for some other reason *before* a final decision is made (e.g., finance is often in a consultation role to projects)
- **Inform**, for the people/groups who are affected by the project but who do not participate in the effort (they are

usually notified of the outcome after the final decisions are made)

Because each organization will divide roles and responsibilities differently, RACI is not a "one size fits all" model. Figure 11.1 shows an example of how you can document the way you would like roles and responsibilities to work, but the specifics will vary for your organization.

Figure 10.1: RACI chart used to define responsibilities

Activity=> Task	Own the LSS Deployment	Identify Projects	Select Projects	Project Results	Project Execution	Team Support	Sustain Changes
Exec Team	A	R	A				
Champion	R	A	R			R	
P&L Management		I		A		R	R
Process Owner		C		R	R	R	A
Black Belt		C		R	R	A	
Tm Leader/Green Belt				R	R		
ETC							

There are a number of key decisions you'll face as you complete a RACI chart. One of them will be determining the balance of power between Black Belts and teams. Black Belts are put in a delicate situation: On the one hand, they have a lot of knowledge that teams and line management can use to make the project a success. On the other hand, if they *impose* their knowledge on those they are helping, they're sending the message that Lean Six Sigma means "do it my way." As a rule, Black Belts should be positioned in the role of *support staff*, not decision-makers, because they are not "experts" in nor do they have any ongoing responsibility for the work.

5. Communicate, communicate, communicate

The cumulative result of different projects focused on cardiac bypass graft surgery at Stanford Hospital and Clinics was that patients could be discharged much sooner and often experienced fewer complications.

But the hospital team soon discovered they had ignored a vital link in patient care: The cardiologists who referred the patients would tell them, "You need a coronary bypass graft. You're going to be in the hospital about nine days." So the patient would go through the surgery and four days later be told they were being sent home. While people aren't typically upset at being released early from the hospital, these patients—expecting a nine day hospital stay—were convinced it was all a cost cutting measure and that they hadn't really gotten their full measure of care. They were also concerned because their family members weren't prepared to take them home at day 4. And that's how Stanford discovered that part of their control plan had to be communicating with anyone who dealt with patients.

This story from Stanford is just one example of why communication is a must-do for managers. Here's another: One reviewer of this book told us confidentially that his company had been involved in Lean Six Sigma for two years. Though he had received some introductory training, no one had ever really explained what was going on and why. Having now read this book, he could understand more about what his company was doing, and he had ideas for using some of the concepts in his own work. He even recalled an incident where a Black Belt had come to him with a question that our reviewer interpreted as a criticism, only to realize now that the Black Belt's intention was quite different.

The managers and others leading a Lean Six Sigma effort face a lot of competing pressures. They have to select and launch projects, make sure training is set up and delivered, provide support to people working on projects, and on and on. But even so, they need to factor in what's going on with the people NOT directly involved in the efforts. They need to put time into creating a web of communication with all parts of the organization:

1) **With bosses**, to make sure everyone understands corporate priorities. Communication with corporate leaders can also be vital in helping to overcome roadblocks or resolve conflicts that may arise between departments.

2) **With project team members**, to make sure they are clear on the purpose, goals, boundaries, and expectations for their project. The manager should also invite communication *from* the team, so they will feel comfortable asking questions, pushing for clarity, and so on.

3) **To and from staff** (and the rest of the organization). In general, the more that employees at all levels are aware of what's going on and why, the more likely they will be to support Lean Six Sigma efforts either directly or indirectly.

6. Support education and training

Lean Six Sigma isn't yet a course in most universities or colleges, let alone high schools. So most people in the workforce—including managers like you—will need to be trained and educated. Managers' responsibilities are to...

- **Educate themselves.** If you want to have role models, try watching what CEOs like Lou Giuliano of ITT Industries and Vance Coffman of Lockheed Martin are doing. Both have participated in their organizations' executive-level training in Lean Six Sigma. You don't have to be a Black Belt—though Graham Richard, the Mayor of Fort Wayne, Indiana, is one!—but you should know enough about Lean Six Sigma so you can ask intelligent questions and guide those involved in projects.

- **Support the education of their staff.**

Conclusion

Lean Six Sigma is a discipline that has learned from past mistakes. And one of the mistakes made by previous improvement methodologies was to ignore management support. Initially, a lot of managers find themselves thinking that Lean Six Sigma efforts are somehow "stealing resources" that they would rather devote to the "real work." But once they see the kinds of *rapid and sustainable* gains earned when well-trained people work on high-priority projects (linked to the managers' business goals), they quickly become enthusiastic supporters of training and education.

In Lean Six Sigma companies, this focus on systems and processes begins at the top. For example, when Lou Giuliano, the CEO of ITT Industries, goes into one of his business units, his first questions for the managers are about what they are doing with their Lean Six Sigma projects—because he knows that it's through these efforts that the company will be able to meet its aggressive goals. This clearly focuses management on process improvement.